C000258003

O ccasionally there is a book which lifts the veil of the past and lets us step into history. IN SEARCH OF ENGLISH GARDENS is that rare thing. With it, we travel through early nineteenth-century England in the opinionated and entertaining company of John Claudius Loudon (1783-1843) and his young wife, Jane. Loudon – creator of the first gardening magazine – was obsessed by a desire to recall the great country parks and gardens of a nation in an era of impending change.

In the 1830s and early 1840s he and his wife journeyed through the countryside, recording with wit and with passion all they saw. His writings allow us to enjoy the magnificence of country houses and their pleasure gardens, the charm of cottages adorned with roses and clematis, even the joys and tribulations of coach travel along narrow country lanes.

We are taken to Blenheim Palace, Alton Towers, Woburn Abbey, Windsor Castle, Stourhead, Chatsworth and Petworth as they were in their heyday. We discover the vanished grandeur of the great gardens of Fonthill, Dropmore and Deepdene. We peer over the hedge into more intimate, personal gardens including Loudon's favourite – Mrs Lawrence's Villa, Drayton Green. We meet a fascinating gallery of characters – innkeepers' daughters, illiterate old gardeners surviving from the Georgian age, pious landlords, genteel widows and young men eager for self-improvement: all with one thing in common, a desire to create the finest garden.

Never brought together in book form, and unavailable for 140 years, his journals are now complemented by 200 illustrations – newly discovered watercolours, historic Victorian photographs, stereoscopics, engravings and sketches that make up a picture of a vanished world, together with botanical prints of plants that Loudon saw and praised.

IN SEARCH OF ENGLISH GARDENS

IN SEARCH OF ENGLISH GARDENS

THE TRAVELS OF JOHN CLAUDIUS LOUDON AND HIS WIFE JANE

EDITED BY PRISCILLA BONIFACE

Lennard Publishing
1987

Lennard Publishing
a division of Lennard Books Ltd
The Old School, Brewhouse Hill
Wheathampstead, Herts AL4 8AN

British Library Cataloguing in Publication Data

Loudon, John Claudius
In search of English gardens : the travels
of John Claudius Loudon and his
wife Jane.
1. Gardens — Great Britain — History —
19th century
I. Title II. Boniface, Priscilla
712'.6'0924 SB466.G7

ISBN 1 85291 000 3

First published 1987
Copyright © this edition and selections Lennard Publishing 1987
Copyright © Introduction and Epilogue Priscilla Boniface 1987

This book is copyright under the Berne Convention
No reproduction without permission
All rights reserved

Designed by Pocknell & Co
Printed in Great Britain by
Butler & Tanner Ltd, Frome and London

CONTENTS

INTRODUCTION

The marriage in 1830 of John Claudius Loudon to Jane Webb created a partnership in which deep and constant affection combined with a determination to instruct the nation on all aspects of gardening. Both wrote prodigiously; both achieved fame from their individual endeavours. But perhaps their most fascinating project, and one that was a real collaboration, was never published as a book. Instead, their marvellously detailed tours of the country, in which they visited 'mansion residences', 'villa residences', villages and towns, recording all that seemed noteworthy, were issued in *The Gardener's Magazine* as a series of articles. More than any other of their works, these tours capture the character of a nation of gardens and gardeners in an era of change. They also make clear to us the nineteenth-century writer's belief that it was a duty to observe, to criticize and to praise, so that all who were in a position to do so might benefit from the author's knowledge.

Through all his works, John Claudius Loudon popularized gardening as an art. It was just one of the ways in which, like those of his similarly high-motivated contemporaries, he sought to improve the human condition. This was made clear in his founding *The Gardener's Magazine* in 1826 'to disseminate new and important information on all topics connected with horticulture and to raise the intellect and the character of those engaged in this art'.

To understand Loudon's vocation, it is important to look at the times that moulded him. Loudon was born near Edinburgh in 1783. His lifetime coincided with a transitional and particularly turbulent phase in the affairs of Britain. The social and economic structure of the country, which until the later eighteenth century had always been predominantly based on agriculture and land-ownership, was breaking up. Newly-emergent industries, many needing to be located in and around urban population centres, were beginning to take the lead in the creation of the nation's wealth, to the detriment of the countryside.

The prolonged Napoleonic Wars, lasting until 1815, exacerbated what was already a difficult situation in rural areas. The attentions of the land-owning aristocracy had been directed to the defence of the realm rather than the good husbandry of their estates. Grain shortages resulted from naval blockades. Then the end of hostilities abroad and the recommencement of imports produced a glut, a reduction in prices, and agricultural depression. These upheavals occurred at a time when the labouring classes on the land were no longer as protected as they had been. The 'bilateral cottage economy' was based on providing service to a landlord in return for sustenance by way of smallholdings and numerous common rights on his lands. Much of the land that had been available for the exercise of various customary rights had been taken away and the rights diminished by Parliamentary Enclosure from around 1760 onwards. The livelihood of cottagers was now further threatened because it became more economic for impoverished landlords to employ labourers day to day than for them to be retained year round. There was much hardship on the great country estates.

Educated in the vibrant intellectual atmosphere of Edinburgh, and gifted with a naturally inquiring mind, Loudon could not help being stimulated into deep and original thought on the condition of the land, both as regards ornament and as regards farming, as soon as he began his self-made career in landscape gardening. This became more obvious as his work led to early travels in Britain. By 1803 he had published his first article, *Observations on Laying out Public Squares*. While working in the south of England, he was struck by one of the many bouts of illness which were to characterize the rest of his life. He rented a farm near Pinner, Middlesex, for his convalescence and invited his father to join him. Together they farmed using methods learned in Scotland. While resident near Pinner, Loudon wrote a pamphlet on his ideas for better farming techniques which attracted considerable attention. It caught the eye of a landowner at Great Tew in Oxfordshire who invited Loudon to lease a farm on his land; there Loudon ran, very successfully, what was in effect England's first agricultural college.

In 1813, eager to learn more of gardening and farming in other countries, Loudon set out on the first of a number of journeys of discovery abroad. It was not the most propitious moment to choose and his lengthy tour through devastated areas of Europe via Poland to Moscow, so soon after Napoleon's retreat, was not without incident. But the quest for further knowledge continued unchecked. By 1820, Loudon had seen many of the formal gardens in France and Italy; they were to influence his views on garden design.

On his return from his travels, Loudon's knowledge was immense, and he began to compile his influential *Encyclopaedia of Gardening*, which was published in 1822. This was a massive book full of pithy descriptions of national styles of gardening, as well as exhaustive analysis of every aspect of practical gardening. Further books included an *Encyclopaedia of Agriculture* (1825) and an *Encyclopaedia of Plants* (1829). In 1826, Loudon started what was to become a life-long task, *The Gardener's Magazine*.

JOHN CLAUDIUS LOUDON.

JANE LOUDON, FROM A MINIATURE.

Jane Webb, meanwhile, had been enjoying the sheltered and prosperous upbringing in Warwickshire that was the lot of the child of a well-to-do Birmingham businessman. She, like John Loudon, had an inquiring mind, one which circumstances allowed to develop. She was educated both by a governess and her own reading, and soon took to writing. Her novel *The Mummy*, published in 1827, when she was 20, was the indirect cause of her meeting John. The book, a striking fantasy set in the twenty-second century, had been reviewed by Loudon in *The Gardener's Magazine*.

It was not so much the plot, telling of an England under the rule of the virgin Queen Claudia in AD 2126, that attracted Loudon to it, but its ingenious and practical descriptions of inventions of the future. Loudon's imagination was particularly seized by Jane's suggestion of mechanised farming. Having mentioned the book in his *Magazine*, he determined to meet its author. A dinner party was arranged by Jane's publisher, and they met in February 1830. Loudon had intended an evening of technical discussion with a like mind. Certainly a like mind was what he encountered, but something rather less predictable took place. As Jane wrote 'It may be easily supposed that he was surprised to find the author of *The Mummy* a woman; but I believe that from that evening he formed an attachment to me, and, in fact, we were married on the 14th of the following September'.

In marrying Loudon, Jane entered a household dominated by gardening, and by writing about it. With customary vigour she set about improving her rudimentary knowledge of gardening. So successful did she eventually become that she was rivalling her husband's literary output. Jane Loudon became especially famous in her own right for her promotion of the art of gardening to ladies, a cause which, not unexpectedly, received the hearty endorsement of her husband. His own, self-imposed workload was now at its most massive: *The Gardener's Magazine* had already been instantly successful; in a short time, four thousand copies of the first issue had been sold. To begin with it was published quarterly, then every two months, and eventually, monthly. It produced an annual income of about £750. The busy office of the *Magazine* was on the ground floor of Loudon's home, at 3 Porchester Terrace in Bayswater, London. Loudon's need of Jane was undoubted: Following the marriage, all his own work was actually written by his devoted wife to his dictation. This was because Loudon's right arm had been amputated in 1825 following a fracture of 1820 which had failed to mend satisfactorily. Together, they worked in the evenings, and often well into the early hours of the morning. In addition to their arduous tours, the couple made many visits to nurseries and to favoured villa residences such as Hendon Rectory, in the environs of London.

As well as their writing, they were much pre-occupied with their own garden at 3 Porchester Terrace and the Reserve Ground which they rented beyond it. Characteristically, Loudon wanted to attempt many different types of gardening, notwithstanding the relatively small space available, even to the extent of planting an arboretum whose size he hoped to contain by rigorous trimming of the roots. Many visitors came, curious to see the home ground of one so quick to comment on the gardens of others.

Life at Porchester Terrace, where John and Jane Loudon occupied a position in cultured London society, was punctuated with intermissions for their travels. There was always much work to catch up with, in office and garden, on their return. Even the birth of their daughter, Agnes in 1832 did not deter the two workaholics from continuing at a relentless pace. There was always so much for the Loudons to write about – they lived in a period of rapid change, and on the pages of *The Gardener's Magazine* many of its causes and effects are chronicled.

Evidence of the agricultural depression was seen by the Loudons in many parts of the countryside of England and Scotland. Railways were starting to be built, changing the landscape and the use that was made of it, as well as patterns of travel. Towns, especially in the Midlands, grew almost overnight. At the same time, the countryside saw those from the professions, commerce, and industry moving into, and occasionally fulfilling a rescue function on, the domains of aristocrats. Loudon visited many of these estates. The lavishly-appointed Deepdene was owned by a banker Thomas Hope, Fonthill Abbey, the fantastic creation of William Beckford, was acquired by an eccentric gunpowder magnate named John Farquhar who relinquished it after the collapse of the famous tower. Farquhar saved another aristocrat from ruin when he bailed out the Marquess of Blandford who had overspent on his estate in Berkshire before moving to Blenheim Palace, which he allowed, according to Loudon, to fall into disarray.

As well as this new bourgeoisie, Loudon was seeking to educate and encourage the fledgling gardening profession. He used the columns of *The Gardener's Magazine* to exhort both employer and employee to seek ways of improving the working conditions and knowledge of gardeners. Jane Loudon wrote after Loudon's death 'I think I never saw Mr. Loudon more pleased than when a highly respectable gardener once told him he was living in a new and most comfortable cottage, which his master had built for him; a noble marquess, who said that he would never have thought of it, but for the observation in Mr. Loudon's

THE LOUDONS' HOUSE IN BAYSWATER, DESIGNED BY LOUDON HIMSELF.

Gardener's Magazine'. Loudon urged employers to provide well-stocked libraries for employees and also to make provision for the education of their dependants. Occasionally, after a particularly satisfying encounter with a gardener, Loudon gave encouragement by giving out copies of useful publications, nearly always written by himself. On many large estates, access for visitors had been accepted practice since the eighteenth century when it had become the fashion to tour estates, guide book in hand. An instance of the withdrawal of this facility at Wilton was, predictably, regretted by Loudon. Loudon dispensed criticism and congratulation as he thought appropriate; the Dukes of Devonshire at Chatsworth and Wellington at Strathfieldsaye received praise but many in the aristocracy were chastised for the run-down appearance of their estates. In this, as in so much else, Loudon apparently gave little thought to any offence his observations might cause.

The upheavals of the period produced a romantic reaction, by those well-removed from the actuality, extolling the supposed virtues of a cottager's life. Roses round the door, neat gardens filled with flowers and vegetables, were seen to indicate that here all was well. Even Loudon, with his well-tuned eye for signs of social injustice, seems at times to have been taken in by these apparent indications of a good life within; whereas a near-contemporary observer of country life, William Cobbett, despite wanting a return to the old country ways, was never fooled.

A pre-occupation with social issues is demonstrated in many passages from *The Gardener's Magazine*; Loudon regrets the impoverished circumstances of inhabitants of places such as Hindon after the Reform Bill, of Flitwick in the wake of the Cato Street conspiracy; and of petty criminals incarcerated in Reading Goal.

Gardening practice was changing too. Predominant in the early nineteenth century had been the 'picturesque' theories of Humphry Repton and Uvedale Price. The poet William Wordsworth favoured gardens which were as uncontrived and natural as possible. Visitors clamoured to see Wordsworth's own garden at Rhydal Mount and his opinions were to influence the planting of many gardens in the Lake District.

In his later years, Repton had moved towards designing multi-style pleasure grounds for clients from the professional and industrial classes, who lived in villa residences rather than huge country houses. Gradually artifice was being allowed to become more obvious. Loudon seems to have had a love/hate relationship with Repton, perhaps, on Loudon's side at least, owing rather more to jealousy that to any great difference of opinion.

Certainly Loudon's theories on the garden landscapes for these new clients, whose taste he sought to form, seem to be a development of Repton's later ideas rather than a major departure from them. It is interesting that in a lot of his tours for *The Gardener's Magazine* Loudon seems irresistibly drawn to many gardens of Repton's design. In Loudon's last years, there was some sort of *rapprochement*, though whether this was genuine or prompted by reasons of economic necessity is not entirely clear.

It was Loudon's contention that a garden should be recognised as a work of art. The beauty of a garden lay in the *mind* of the beholder; it was necessary for humans to be educated to know what they were seeing before it could be fully appreciated. He believed that the display of the characteristics of an individual plant was of greater importance than an overall garden scheme. This plantsman's style of gardening became known as 'gardenesque'. Flower gardens, formerly banished to the extremities of a pleasure ground, were now increasingly being installed around a villa residence. The renowned flower garden at Dropmore for example was visited and admired by Loudon.

During the nineteenth century, many 'new' plants and shrubs were being imported and displayed in gardens throughout Britain. This was another reason for the move towards the gardenesque style. Loudon refers to the China Rose; it had been introduced into Britain in the late eighteenth century and was present in a number of gardens. Other new introductions mentioned include the, now commonplace, Magnolia soulangiana, and Araucaria imbricata. Descriptions of gardens as 'American' or 'Chinese', indicated the origin of the plants themselves rather than styles of garden design. Assemblages defined by plant type, such as arboretums – a term used by Repton –, herbariums, and pinetums, were popular. The black Italian poplar, once introduced, apparently quickly become as widespread in plantations as conifers are in Britain today.

Many of the tender plants from abroad could not withstand the British climate so they were housed in glasshouses. There, too, fruits were forced for the table. Loudon was in the forefront of experimentation with glasshouse design and in his travels he was keen to see how glasshouses were being constructed and managed. It must have been with mixed feelings that he surveyed Joseph Paxton's innovatory and celebrated Great Stove at Chatsworth.

IMPLEMENTS OF GARDENING.

As a designer, Loudon was naturally interested in house interiors as well as their gardens. *The Gardener's Magazine* carries a detailed description of the accoutrements of Whitmore Lodge, the villa belonging to a Mr. Mangles; whereas rooms at Goodwood were approved, those at Arundel Castle were not. Everywhere, inside and out, Loudon was impressed with neatness and tidiness. To such he attached great importance, exemplified in his own house and garden. In so doing he revealed a preoccupation, traditional to the class from which he came and which, in the main, he sought to guide. Through the medium of *The Gardener's Magazine*, Loudon could give reassurance to the newly-rich whose correspondingly new tastes were unsure and largely unformed.

Loudon regarded it as his duty to include a large amount of his own verbiage in the *Magazine*. In 1836 he wrote, without humour or modesty, 'It would be far easier for us to fill this Magazine with papers by our correspondents, on the cultivation of particular plants or crops, than to write long articles in it ourselves; but we are guided in selecting, preparing, or writing articles for publication, solely by what we consider to be the wants of our readers, whether practical gardeners, or their employers'.

Jane Loudon accompanied her husband on his demanding tours, providing professional and wifely support; latterly, their daughter Agnes went with them. At first they travelled by one-horse phaeton, but later they used railways. Occasionally Jane would remain in one place or return home while her husband carried out a commission for a client. Loudon's celebrity was such that many receptions were arranged in his honour during the course of his tours.

Their tour of the north of England and Scotland in 1831 was interrupted by a dash south because Loudon's mother, who lived at 5 Porchester Terrace, was dying. Loudon's own life was punctuated by bouts of ill-health which he did his best to ignore; in 1841 however, he was forced to halt a tour for six weeks in Scotland.

The tone of his writing changes from tour to tour. One senses the happy mood of the pair on their travels in 1832 when Jane was pregnant. Also apparent is the pleasure that was induced in Loudon by a return to his native soil in 1841 – notwithstanding an aside about the meanness of his countrymen. When Loudon was feeling unwell, he could turn particularly waspish. Yet the tour to the West Country in 1842, when he had scarcely more than a year to live, has an elegiac quality; every page seems awash with sunshine, and scented by the lemon trees which seemed to flourish in Devon and Cornwall at that time.

In 1843, John suffered inflammation of the lungs. Coincidentally, his work included the task of advising on the design of cemeteries – in Bath and Southampton and in writing a book *On the Laying Out, Planting and Managing Cemeteries and the Improvement of Churchyards*. By this time, the Loudons were in an impecunious state. This knowledge encouraged John to work at fever pitch until the end. He died literally on his feet, with his wife Jane's arms around him, on 14 December, 1843.

The complete works of Loudon's tours, as printed in *The Gardener's Magazine* comprise some 400,000 words. I have had to reduce this bulk to about 55,000 words to keep within the constraints of a modern illustrated book of manageable size in what has been a difficult editorial task of selection.

POLISH GARDENS FROM THE *ENCYCLOPAEDIA OF GARDENING.*

One of my main concerns has been to produce a readable book entirely from Loudon's very considerable output so, to avoid over-fragmentation of the chosen portions, I have taken the liberty of running together separated passages without indicating the breaks. In a very few cases, passages published out of chronological order within a tour, or published later than the tour from which they derived, have been inserted in an appropriate place. The order here therefore makes sense of the tours chronologically rather than reflects the date of publication.

Changes to the text are minimal. New words are enclosed in square brackets. I have made a few minor changes to the punctuation to achieve links and/or remove ambiguities, and have changed some lower case letters to capital letters and vice versa, for similar reasons; but inconsistencies of spelling (Ellestree for example) and names of counties remain as originally printed. My aim has been to clarify for the modern reader while changing as little as possible of the selected, original text.

While the emphasis is on Loudon's appreciation of English gardens, I thought it important to include some descriptions of Scotland, not just because Loudon was a Scot, but also because such passages give an impression of the range of the original, especially as Loudon made comparisons between the two national styles of gardening.

Here, the text is complemented with contemporary illustrations where possible. The prints by E. Adveno Brooke date from the 1850s and have been chosen to show gardens that remained in essence as Loudon described them; a few early photographs have also been used. Again the intention has been to show the gardens as they looked when Loudon saw them.

Loudon was at pains to include as much as possible in *The Gardener's Magazine* for his readers' edification. Now, to those accustomed to information in photographic form, his descriptions may occasionally seem almost absurdly long. It should be remembered that he had little option but to describe every blade of grass if he was to get his message, much of which was new, across to his readers.

In making this selection, therefore, I have tried to retain the 'flavour' of the original, to be true to the character of Loudon and to the time in which he lived, even to the extent of including some passages which may seem to later twentieth-century taste florid and verbose. I hope that my selection reveals to a new audience the 'essential' Loudon, conveying something of his significance as a 'new professional' in a world of emergent professionalism and of his personality in that very contemporary phenomenon, a husband and wife team.

Priscilla Boniface
June, 1987

1

HERTFORDSHIRE, BEDFORDSHIRE, BERKSHIRE, SURREY, SUSSEX AND MIDDLESEX

JULY – AUGUST 1829

LONDON TO FLITWICK HOUSE. JULY 22. — It happens that the most direct route from Bayswater to Flitwick House is by secondary roads and lanes, so quiet and rural, that such a proprietor as the Duke of Bedford, riding along them, might fancy himself on his own estate. As we passed Cannons, at Edgeware, the magnificent and truly aristocratic idea of the Duke of Chandos recurred to our mind, viz. that of having a straight avenue from his house here to his house in Cavendish Square, a distance of above nine miles, entirely on his own estate. Had he lived but a few years longer, it is said he would have realised the idea, as he had succeeded in purchasing every thing necessary but for a small spot at Paddington.

The magnificence of the house is still talked of by the old people in the neighbourhood. The principal staircase consisted of blocks of Italian marble, 20 ft. long, and the handrailing was of silver. This house has long since been pulled down, but the lodges at the entrance gates still exist, and are so ample in their dimensions, and commodious within, as to have been let, at different times, as country-houses, to gentlemen of the rank of esquires, magistrates, and officers in the army and navy. The duke had a horse-patrol, which perambulated the boundaries of the park, by night and day; a body-guard; a band of music for general purposes, and one or two eminent musicians for joining them on grand occasions, and leading the church music.

No outlet from London has been more improved within the last fifteen years than the road to Edgeware, which, from passing through naked grass fields, with, here and there, a miserable cottage, farm-house, or a hay barn, is now bordered by villas and gardens, vying with each other in architectural taste, in the display of flowers, exotic trees and shrubs, and in what no foreigner can form an idea of who has not been in the country, English turf and gravel.

The road from Edgeware to St. Albans is very retired, and almost wholly pastoral or agricultural. Some few of the cottages and gardens which border it appear comfortable; but not many. The doors of those of the lowest class were open, and we could see mothers and their children seated at little tables, with cups and saucers and a small loaf before them, but without a table-cloth; the men, doubtless, at work in the fields, had carried with them their bread and bacon. The landlord of the public-house at Ellestree, a man apparently more than usually religious, described to us the manner in which three men had, ten days before, been drowned in the reservoir. Four companions, somewhat intoxicated, went to take a sail on the Sunday afternoon, and fell overboard; only one of them, who could swim, was saved. They were single men, and bad characters; and the parish, he observed, would be rather a gainer by their loss than otherwise. How dreadful to have such a tribute to one's memory paid by a neighbour! The very idea of it seems enough to reform a man. A new inn in the outskirts of St. Albans, in the Dunstable road, has an ample garden, not made the most of. Such a piece of ground, and a gardener of taste, would give an inn so situated so great a superiority, that every body would be tempted to stop there; but the garden of this Boniface exhibits but the beginning of a good idea. Every thing that creates an allusion to home ought to be encouraged at an inn; and therefore, every place of entertainment, from the smallest hedge-alehouse upwards, ought to have a large garden, a library more or less extensive, a book of country maps, a road-book, a Shakspeare, a Don Juan (purified copies, of course), a newspaper, and one periodical or more.

THE ROAD FROM ST ALBANS TO EDGEWARE.

The very small village of Flitwick is composed of as miserable cottages as any in England; the inhabitants, following no manufacture, and having very little agricultural employment, derive a great part of their scanty subsistence from the poor-rates. The men are said to be almost all poachers, and three fourths of them, we were told, had been on the tread-wheel; some had been transported, one belonged to the Cato Street conspiracy, and one or two have been hanged. At church, on Sunday (July 26.), very few men attended, and the congregation consisted chiefly of young women and children, by no means healthy for a country population. We were not much surprised at hearing two marriages announced; for, when mankind are in a state of degradation and suffering, there is nothing to restrain them from doing all they incline to do; and every thing will be resorted to that has any chance of procuring present enjoyment, without reference to future consequences. The marriages of

21

WOBURN ABBEY – 'THE COMMANDING POSITION OF THE HOUSE.'

poor people are always prolific in children; they do not always grow up; but their births and deaths are at least food for the church, as poaching is for the magistracy and the lawyers. The clergyman had an excellent discourse on contentment, and against covetousness!

FLITWICK HOUSE; JOHN THOMAS BROOKS, ESQ. — [is] a pattern of order and judicious arrangement. The proprietor is a warm-hearted man, a kind and liberal master, and a great friend to gardeners and gardening. Both the grounds and house have been materially improved and the whole continues to maintain its high character for good keeping. A public road has been changed in direction, which, while it has added to the beauty and free unrestrained air of the scenery, has, of course, increased the value of the property.

WOBURN ABBEY; THE DUKE OF BEDFORD. JULY 28. — The fine circumstances at Woburn Abbey are, the extent and variety of surface of the park, its unequalled oak groves and evergreen plantations, the commanding situation of the house, the judicious distance and good effect in the view of the village of Woburn, and the beauty of certain pieces of water, as seen from the house. Add to these established features the more recent ones of the grass garden, thornery, nursery, the Northumbrian farm, dairy, aviary, the sculpture galleries, heathery, the very complete kitchen-garden now forming, the salicetum, rockwork, flower-gardens, children's gardens, and other improvements in the pleasure-ground; and the ornamental cottages, with their gardens, in the outskirts of the park.

The collection of heaths, hardy and exotic, is the most complete in the world, and not less so the collection of willows. The present duke is a scientific botanist, and a great lover of gardening and the fine arts, as his predecessor was of agriculture.

The kitchen-garden, since our visit in February is rapidly advancing towards completion, and will be one of the first in England. The effect even surpasses expectation; the head-gardener or his wife, sitting in the parlour by the fire, can now, without any change of

22

position, see through one window over the whole of the garden, in front of the hot-houses; and through the other window, over the whole of the triple range of pine, melon, and forcing-pits behind the range. Experience proves that this power of inspection is something more than an imaginary advantage. The gardener's house is altogether one of the best we have seen; it does honour to the feelings of the duke, who thus evinces a wish to see his upper servants not only comfortable and healthy, but living in a comparatively elegant and respectable style; and to Mr. Atkinson, his architect, for so completely embodying the duke's wishes. We could name a duke, the whole of whose head-gardener's shed, chimney-top included, in which the gardener keeps a tall young wife, and one or two children, might be erected in the parlour referred to. There is no class of gentlemen's servants so badly lodged as gardeners generally are; but, while we state this, it is proper to mention, at the same time, that the fault is very often owing to the gardener not making known his wants. Henceforth let every gardener speak out candidly and respectfully to his employer, and thus avoid the temptation of speaking harshly of him without reason, and of generating and nourishing bad feelings on either side.

There is a handsome flower-garden here, designed by the present duchess; and near it is the most magnificent sculpture gallery to be found in any private house in England; the lofty and ample conservatory, the heathery, the botanic stoves, flower-houses, florist's garden, and a veranda of nearly a quarter of a mile in length, leading to the tennis-court, dairy, &c. We could not help constrasting the magnificence of the garden scenery and orangery with the meagre effect of those we had lately seen at Windsor; but we consoled ourselves by reflecting, that there being but one king, his example could be but of little

WOBURN ABBEY – 'THE MAGNIFICENT SCULPTURE GALLERY...AND THE LOFTY
CONSERVATORY.'

23

consequence; whereas we have many country gentlemen of knowledge and taste possessing seats of different degrees of magnificence and beauty to raise and maintain the character of the country. So long, indeed, as we have such noblemen as the Dukes of Bedford, Northumberland, Portland, Buccleugh, Devonshire, &c., and such commoners as Mr. Hope of Deepdene, Mr. Wells of Redleaf, Mr. Coke of Holkham, Mr. Barclay, Mrs. Marryatt, &c., we need not fear the example of a British king, of the late palace at Kew, the modern one at Pimlico, or the gardens at these places, and at Windsor. What we greatly admire at Woburn is, the perfect order and keeping of every part of the place, from the little cast-iron margins of the squares of grasses, the box edgings to the small beds of hardy heaths, or the hen-coops in the aviary, to the approach roads, park wall, trees, and plantations. The order and neatness are every where perfect, and this perfection is produced by *division* of duties, and by assigning to every division rather too many than too few to perform its labours. One leading manager sees that the duties of every division is properly performed; the divisions are checks or stimuli to one another, and the duke and the public are stimuli to the manager and the whole. The grand secret of the plan of all this is the division of duties; and the secret of the execution, the *abundance of hands* to perform them. Let this principle be borne in mind by every master. Nine tenths of the slovenliness about gentlemen's seats arises from a want of sufficient hands; from attempting more than there is means adequate to perform.

It is but justice to the late Mr. Repton to say, that much of the scenic beauty of the views from Woburn Abbey may be traced to his suggestions for the formation of pieces of water.

WHITMORE LODGE, NEAR SUNNING HILL; ROBERT MANGLES, ESQ. AUGUST 2. — We have before noticed this place as very highly kept; it is still equally so, and has been greatly improved by additions to the house and by alterations in the grounds. Mr. Mangles has a very marked taste for symmetry in architecture, and for order and contrivance in interior arrangement; fitting up, as the upholsterer terms it, and finishing and furnishing; and he is happy in finding the counterpart of his own tastes in Mrs. Mangles. The interior of the house, therefore, it may easily be conceived, is a perfect museum of contrivances, excellent furniture, and rare, precious, or curious articles. We have examined every corner of the house, from the cellar to the bed-rooms, and shall shortly enumerate a few things from recollection.

Cellar. The bins divided by slate, to save room. The French portable ice vessel found to preserve the ice for a number of days after it is taken from the ice-house.

Kitchen. The walls lined with Dutch tiles, which, being glazed, do not retain the dust, and they are always clean. The cook said they rendered the place too hot. Instead of charcoal stoves for compound cookery, one immense cast-iron plate is heated on the principle of a common hot-house flue, by a common coal fire below. Steaming-closet and oven very perfect. Cistern behind the fire, which, by communicating-pipes heats a bath. Ventilation openings near the floor, and near the ceiling, and through wire grating to exclude flies.

Out-house. Knife-cleaning machine. Wheel-brush for brushing shoes and the common description of clothes.

China closet. Very complete collection; the walls covered with paper, in imitation of

NEAR ST ALBANS

A FÊT

GOODWOOD – IN THE GROUNDS

GOODWOOD – A VIEW OF THE RACES

Dutch tiles. Here we have forgot something we intended to notice.

Entrance-hall and garden-front saloon. Sunk panels in the floor, for the large mats, 6 ft. square, to allow of the doors opening over them. A raised bed for flowers in the centre of the garden saloon, with stone curb. A large recess in the wall, enclosed with brass wire, serves as an aviary for canary birds; the birds pass through small unconspicuous openings on one side of the recess to their eating and drinking place, so that no husks of seeds are ever seen from the saloon. Shutters double and curiously contrived both for warmth and security. In the flower-bed is now a collection of handsome balsams, the pots covered with green moss.

Mr. Mangles' dressing-room and business-room. Clothes-press admirably arranged; the drawers containing the different parts of dress, named and numbered. Complete system of housekeeping books; letters and copying machine; engraved forms of bankers' checks; with the family arms, view of the house, &c.

Breakfast-room. The walls covered with brown moreen, bordered by gimp, with cable cord in the angles. Egyptian fire-irons, ornaments, tables, &c., from the late sale at White Knights, of the Duke of Marlborough's rarities. Frames to mirror, doors, &c., of bird's eye maple, and corresponding patterns.

Dining-room. Slips of lead, three-sided, and covered with oil cloth, laid along the skirting on the carpet, to prevent the chairs from being pushed too near to the wall. Contrivance for receiving the dinner hot, direct from the kitchen, as at Arundel Castle, and said to be also at Dreghorn Castle, near Edinburgh. Large bay window for the dessert table during the summer season.

Drawing-room. The whole of the light admitted from a bay of three large windows. Bird-cage, with an under-story, in which the bird descends through a small opening; by a trap-ladder, to its eating-place, so that no husks of seeds are ever exposed to view. Flower-stand, in which cut flowers are kept in moist sand. Set of musicians in Dresden china, numerous other articles of virtu, &c.

Staircase, &c., heated by a Brussels stove, which is of iron, cased inside with fire-stone, very handsome and effective.

Bed-rooms. Three sorts of blinds are in use; the best kind seems to be that in which the cloth is rolled up by pulling a string which coils up and unrolls in a groove on the end of the roller. The end of the string hangs loose.

What is particularly deserving of imitation in this house is the admission of light into all the rooms, not by rows of windows, but by bays or large windows without any cross lights, so that the light always comes in masses, and thus sets off all forms to advantage. There is not a room in the house with two windows, nor a door with a display of locks, knobs, handles, and other fastenings, as if, in a house of enjoyment, the security of person or property were a matter of constant consideration. The view of the pleasure-ground from the dining-room displays a plain lawn, ornamented with shrubs and trees, but without flowers; that from the breakfast-room the same view, but introducing an inviting portion of extreme distance; that from the drawing-room, a lawn highly enriched with baskets of flowers of different shapes, grouped so as to exhibit handsome combinations; a large one being directly in front, two irregular ones at each side along the walk, and a smaller regular one placed beyond the first at some little distance.

Independently of the beauty and high keeping of Whitmore Lodge, it is interesting, as affording an example of a small villa that would gain nothing in character or effect by additional acres. All the views are to the south and east, over an extensive, richly-wooded country, and terminating in the south-west in the hilly parts of Bagshot Heath. Mr. Gilpin, whose professional assistance was called in, some years ago, when the property was purchased, and Mr. Mangles, have managed the foreground so as completely to appropriate all beyond it; and were the possessor now to have an opportunity of rendering the whole landscape his property, though he might add to his power and consequence, he could not add to the beauty of his residence. The important lesson to be learned from all this is the great advantage of building and gardening in elevated situations. The proprietor of thousands of acres, whose establishment requires a baronial mansion, may form his park on a flat surface, elevate his house by a terraced platform, and look from the centre to the circumference, over a home-made landscape; but the smaller gentleman, if he is a man of taste, will make choice of the top or the side of a hill, where he can command an extensive prospect, at least on two sides, and where one acre will go as far, in point of enjoyment and picturesque effect of scenery and sky, as a hundred acres on a plain decorated with all the art of the architect and the landscape-gardener.

WINGFIELD SPA, IN WINDSOR FOREST (4 miles from Windsor, and 4½ from Maidenhead). AUGUST 4. — A spring has been discovered here, of which it is said "that the quantity of muriate of magnesia being greater than is usually met with, and its being conjoined with sulphate of magnesia and sulphate of soda, render it superior to Cheltenham water." A rustic pump-room from a design by Mr. Mangles, has been erected over it; extensive walks, formed in the copse woods around it; and hard by, a spacious mansion, late the residence of Captain Forbes, R.N., has been opened as a hotel and boarding-house, on reasonable terms. The situation being desirable in point of distance from London, and in a country affording abundant food for the botanist, and the lover of the picturesque, we should hope it will succeed. The patronage of some distinguished person would be a useful beginning. Two or three poor nobles of high fashion might have the run of the hotel and spa for the summer, in

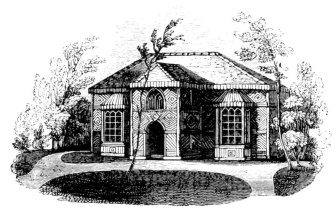

WINGFIELD SPA – 'A RUSTIC PUMP-ROOM FROM A DESIGN BY MR MANGLES.'

consideration of their coming to the hotel in bad health, taking the waters, and finding the greatest benefit from them.

SANDPIT GATE, AUGUST 4. — The effect on entering is very grand, and the castellated lodge is not unsuitable to a royal forest. Near the gate are some miserable-looking wooden hovels, containing the king's menagerie. This was not the state-day for seeing the giraffe; but we had a glimpse of the noble animal through the large chinks of the weather-boarding of the old barn in which he is lodged; he appears thin, sickly, and very inferior to the giraffe of the Jardin des Plantes.

BAGSHOT PARK; THE DUKE OF GLOUCESTER. AUGUST 5. — The flower-garden here is in as complete order as it was when we first viewed it in May, 1828. The scene which struck us with most force during this visit was the American ground, in which the tufted masses of peat-earth shrubs, magnolias, rhododendrons, andromedas, azaleas, kalmias, ericas, &c., looked admirably. As minor subjects of interest we noticed the following: — Amaryllis purpurea, now Theolota purpurea, flowers all the season. The large plants of Hydrangea, in the common loam of the place, always come with blue flowers; but small cuttings taken from the same plants in June, after the flower buds are formed, and rooted and the flowers expanded in July and August in pots of the smallest size, invariably have the flowers red. It would thus appear necessary that the sap should circulate through the roots, or through the whole of a large plant, before it partakes of the quality which renders it blue. In the greenhouse is a large Fuchsia coccinea, covered all the season with such an abundance of berries, that tarts might be made of them if they were considered eatable. These berries drop

BAGSHOT PARK – 'THE FLOWER-GARDEN HERE IS IN AS COMPLETE AN ORDER AS IT WAS WHEN WE FIRST VIEWED IT IN 1828.'

BAGSHOT PARK, THE MOSS HOUSE.

and produce good plants the same season; from which it would appear that the Fuchsia might be treated as a half-hardy annual, and raised from seed every spring in hot-beds along with Marigolds and China asters, and transplanted in the borders.

The kitchen-garden here has a ruinous appearance; the forcing-houses seem to be tumbling down, and the tops of the walls would require to be weeded as well as the walks, which is the case, as we are informed, with the garden walls of that fine old place, Longleat. Notwithstanding these disadvantages, Mr. Smith continues to raise good crops of various articles. There is a bee-house with a good many hives, for the purpose of producing glasses of fresh honey every day; they are under the care of an enthusiastic and enlightened bee- master, once a lieutenant in the navy.

BAGSHOT PARK, THE ORANGERY.

KNAPP HILL NURSERY; MR. WATERER. AUGUST 6. — We had heard much in London, and from various gardeners in the country, of the splendid collection of new seedling azaleas which flowered here in June last, not one of which is yet given out to the trade; but, of course, at this season we could only see the foliage. Among other things we noted Andromeda arborea, 10ft. high, and finely in flower; Vaccinium Arctostaphylos, the Madeira bilberry, 6ft. high, and richly covered with fruit; another species, unknown, bearing very large fruit. Both species well deserve culture, where peat earth is not scarce, as fruits for tarts and for eating with cream, like other bilberries. Magnolia auriculata, very luxuriant; measured one of the leaves, and found it 22in. long, and 11in. wide. Lilium superbum, 10ft. high, coming into flower. The great art in getting this species to flower well, as Mr. Cameron of Bury Hill informed us, is to keep the bulbs single, by taking them up, separating, and replanting. It is evident that, by this practice, the greatest possible supply of nourishment will be obtained by each plant. Phlox Thomsoni, a new variety, in flower. Daphnia collina, a variety with striped leaves. This nursery excells in the management of hedges, which are in some cases 8 or 10ft. high, and not more than 8 or 10in. thick: but, in general, it is not quite so neat and orderly as we could wish; and though we have never seen the weeds exceed the economic point, we would rather see weeding carried lower. We never yet knew a nursery or market-garden, where any money was made, that was not kept *orderly,* at all events, and most of them even *neatly.* We do not say that much is wanting at Knapp Hill; but still we should like to see both principles pushed farther; a good many of the old things grubbed up, the walks and compartments more correctly lined out, and no weeds ever suffered to grow above an inch high. We hint this with the more confidence, knowing that Mr. Waterer will take it in good part, and that it will be in his favour with the hundreds of gardeners and gentlemen that will come from all quarters next June to see the bloom of new azaleas.

AUGUST 7. We met Mr. John Damper Parks, late gardener to the Earl of Arran, at Bognor, and at one time Voyaging Botanist to the Horticultural Society. He had just left his place, and was on a walking botanical excursion, calling at all the interesting gardens on his way, and gathering the more rare wild plants, and examining them, by *Galpine's Compendium.* Mr. Parks is a good botanist and gardener, and a prudent man. He was sent to China by the Horticultural Society some years ago, and gave us a good deal of curious information as to the customs and garden culture of that country; but we will not plough with the Society's heifer, but rather repeat our approbation of Mr. Parks' mode of travelling through the country on foot, and procuring information in his profession; and recommend to all gardeners, whether in or out of place, to call and see other gardens as frequently and extensively as they possibly can. We can assure them from the experience of others as well as our own, that they will, if they are men of any observation, learn more in a week spent in this way, than in a year of close attention, and even reading at home. We would lend our head gardener a horse, perhaps a velocipede might do, and allow him so much a day, say 20s., for a certain number of days in every year, and oblige him to make tours, and write in a journal, to be kept in the garden library, where he had been, and what he had seen.

STROUD HOUSE, NEAR HASLEMERE; MISS PERRY. AUGUST 8. — A small villa exhibiting a perfect model of order and neatness in the house and grounds, and quiet, elegant, rural retirement in the family. The road from Godalming to Haslemere, a distance of eight miles, is one of the most grand and romantic in Surrey or Sussex. It is chiefly through natural woods and open woody commons, and it passes over two or three hills, from the highest of which, between Stroud and Haslemere, a very extensive prospect is obtained. Stroud House is built in a glade in the skirt of an extensive natural oak copse near the road, with a lawn in front and behind, the kitchen-garden and offices at one side, and an orchard and gardener's cottage at the other. Two or three paddocks or ploughed fields, and extensive copse woods, with a winding brook and circuitous walk complete the leading features. The keeping of the lawn, and every thing about the house, is as high and perfect as any thing we have ever seen; and the walks in the copse are kept as clean, dry, and open as copse walks can be. The various bridges over the brooks, and the consequent turns of the walk; the glimpses of the water and broken banks, caught here and there through the trees; the numerous wild plants, abundance of pheasants, singing birds, butterflies, dragon flies in their season, owls in the evening, &c. constitute the attractions of the wood. The house was formed by additions and alterations to an old structure by John Perry, Esq. the proprietor, an architect in Godalming, who has

STROUD HOUSE – 'A SMALL VILLA EXHIBITING A PERFECT MODEL OF ORDER AND NEATNESS...'

distinguished himself by several meritorious erections there and in the surrounding country. Among other contrivances in the interior which deserve to be mentioned, are bell-pulls in every room, which communicate with a bell placed at the head of the gardener's bed, in his adjoining cottage. The communication of the wire from the house to the cottage is through a leaden pipe, sunk some feet under ground, and protected by brick-work, so that no intended housebreaker could easily dig down to it and cut it off. In the evening, this bell serves to call the gardener, who is married, when he may be wanted for any domestic purpose, and, in the night time, serves as an alarm. The family here consists of five sisters of highly cultivated minds; our reason for mentioning which is, to refer to them as an example of what may be attained to in botany by self-instruction, without a single hint of any kind from a botanist, or any person knowing the names of plants. Three of these ladies are acute systematic botanists, and discover the name of every British plant in flower which comes in their way, from Galpine's *Compendium,* and every exotic from the *Encyclopædia of Plants;* and one of them has commenced a series of outlines of British plants, nearly, or wholly, as large as life, so accurate and characteristic, that Mr. Don, of the Linnean Society, who has seen some of them, says they have seldom been equalled, and never surpassed. We hope they may one day be engraved and published; though we cannot help stating, that the pleasure of discovering the names of plants from descriptions, as now done by the Misses Perry, must be much greater than the lazy enjoyment of identifying them with engravings of any kind. The labour is greater, and the reward is as the labour. The Misses Perry were the first who introduced the practice of archery into this part of the country, about fifteen years ago, and it is now become general in the neighbourhood among ladies.

The gardener here, Arthur Morrey, is a most industrious and valuable man, and every thing under his charge does him great credit. He also has two boys and four girls, healthy children, to each of whom we have sent a school-book, and, to the father, a pair of French *sabots* for putting over his shoes in the pruning season. We would strongly recommend these *sabots* (wooden shoes) to all journeymen gardeners, as most valuable for keeping their feet dry and warm while standing on wet ground pruning trees in the winter or spring season. They may be had through any London or Edinburgh nurseryman, who may easily procure them from any sea-port on the Continent, and they are very cheap and durable. Indeed, we are of the opinion that every head-gardener ought to keep a stock of them for the use of the men under his care, in the same way as he keeps spades, rakes, and other tools. Nurserymen and gentlemen's gardeners find that it pays to warm, by a flue or a steam-pipe, the back sheds in which their men work in the winter time. Why should it not, also, pay to keep their workmen's feet dry and warm when they are working in the open air at that season? To begin the thing, we hereby offer a copy of our *Hortus Britannicus* to the first head-gardener in England who shall, with the consent of his employer, procure 20 pairs of *sabots* from a London nurseryman, for the use of his men; the like stimulus to the first gardener in Scotland, the *sabots* being procured from an Edinburgh nurseryman; and the like for Ireland, the *sabots* being procured from a Dublin nurseryman. We are desirous that the *sabots* should be procured from nurserymen, in order that these may get into the way of keeping a stock of them; and we shall be glad to know the nurserymen's names, that we may publish them for the benefit of gardeners generally.

PETWORTH HOUSE; THE EARL OF EGREMONT. AUGUST 11. — This is in many respects a very noble place. The house stands close to, and indeed may be said to form a part of, the town. In the angle of a narrow street is situated the principal entrance, from whence the visitor, leaving a small porter's lodge, passes through low cloisters to a noble saloon in the centre of an extensive suite of rooms; these rooms look on the park, and have no fault in our eyes but that of being three of four feet too low in the floor for dignity of effect, in consequence of which the view to the park is less commanding. This view contains a large piece of water, a wooded hill to the right, a portion of distance to the left, a church steeple beyond a wood in the centre, and is, on the whole, as well managed and as striking as a view over a surface which does not fall away from the house, as at Woburn Abbey for example, can be. The park, the walls of which are said to be twelve miles in circumference, is well stocked with deer, cattle, sheep, and pigs, and once contained buffaloes, quaggas, zebras, wild horses, asses, and other quadrupeds. On remarking to the person who showed us the rooms on the quantity of pigs grazing in front of the windows, and on the number of townsmen playing at skittles beside them, she observed, that the earl, her master, took delight in seeing every living thing enjoying its existence; an expression indicative of a character which greatly pleases us; for what can be more gratifying than to see a rich man giving undeniable proofs that he wishes not only to share the bounties of Providence with his poorer neighbours, but to reflect them back as it were upon all nature! In the house are a number of excellent pictures, both of ancient and modern masters; and what is always satisfactory to hear, because it leads to the mutual improvement of patrons and artists, most of the modern pictures were painted during the stay of the artist in the house. Among the sculptures is a marble bust of the celebrated Arthur Young, the earl having frequently consulted him respecting his agricultural improvements.

In [one] garden court is a large standard fig-tree, which bears tolerable crops annually, without any care whatever, though it can have very little sun after two o'clock in the day. In a conservatory in this court there is a lemon tree, trained against the back wall, which, in consequence of Mr. Harrison's mode of pruning, bears large crops, and has all the year fruit of different sizes, together with blossoms.

In this garden a tortoise has lived for many years; it is fed on the leaves of lettuce, &c. occasionally, but derives the greater part of its food from the grass and plants with which it is surrounded. In winter it buries itself in the soil below the depth to which the frost penetrates. In a third court is a small flower-garden recently formed, and a Pelargonium house containing a variety of new sorts raised here from seeds. The beds of the flower-garden are planted with the choicest new half-hardy annuals, such as verbena Melindres, Clarkia pulchella, Salvia splendens, and also a new variety of this Salvia raised here from seed, and of which a drawing was made for us by Miss Sarah Perry. On the north side of the house the shrubbery commences, and consists of a walk with glades of turf, shrubs, and lofty trees on each side, among which are some fine old hollies and four silver firs of extraordinary dimensions. Farther on is an open grove of various trees, among which are twelve large silver firs, and a Grecian temple, commanding an extensive prospect.

There are sixteen acres in the kitchen-garden here, besides eight acres of slip and of orchard. Mr. Harrison, as the head manager, has one of his sons as a foreman, and all the rest of the men are common country labourers. A regular scientific gardener as a foreman is essential in such a place as this; and there should also be a regular-bred gardener to attend to the small gardens, and greenhouses at the house, if it were only for the purpose of telling any stranger that asks him the names of the plants. The poor fellow who is the master of that department at present, being, as he informed us, *no scollard,* and unable either to read or write, makes sad havoc with the scientific names, and it is impossible that Mr. Harrison or his son can always be in the way.

On the whole, we were very much gratified with the house, the grounds, and the gardens, all of which, especially the kitchen-garden, were in the most perfect order. We shall not attempt to present any thing to Mr. Harrison in the way of encouraging him; but we hope his noble and benevolent employer will present his son with the *Magazine of Natural History* in our name. We must take the further liberty of stating, that we do not think it altogether creditable to a nobleman of the Earl of Egremont's wealth and good character to have the people about him so utterly ignorant as the mass of them appear to be. It would not cost much either of trouble or money, to establish proper schools and libraries all over His Lordship's estate in this part of the country, and to lay down a rule to be acted upon by all managers and upper servants, and which would soon be voluntarily imitated by all the farmers and tradesmen; viz. that no man of woman, born after the year 1826, should be employed, who could not produce a certificate from one of these schools, or otherwise show that there or elsewhere he or she had received a competent stock of school education, and could at least read, write, cipher, measure land and work, and draw. In the mean time, we think a garden library should be formed, and Mr. Harrison encouraged to take young men, as at Welbeck and other places, in order to initiate them in his practices, and produce a few good gardeners for a part of the country which seems at present to be very much in want of them.

Westdean House; Lord Selsey. August 13. — Westdean House is situated near the bottom of one of those flat dry valleys which are common in chalky countries. The spot is by no means marked by Nature, and perhaps something more might have been done by art, in the

WESTDEAN HOUSE – 'SITUATED NEAR THE BOTTOM OF ONE OF THOSE FLAT DRY
VALLEYS WHICH ARE COMMON IN CHALKY COUNTRIES.'

WESTDEAN HOUSE – 'THE SPOT IS BY NO MEANS MARKED BY NATURE, AND
PERHAPS SOMETHING MORE MIGHT HAVE BEEN DONE BY ART.'

way of a terraced basement, to enhance that which is fixed on. However, an exceedingly good, plain, Gothic house is built; and as the views from it cannot be rendered striking, from the absence of natural features and water, they are at least pleasing. According to the momentary impression made during our hasty glance, the carriage entrance ought to have been in the other front, which, being without distant view, would have left what interest there is in the distant scenery to have surprised the visitor from the windows of the garden front. This mode of entering a house from the front containing the best views, is in our opinion a prevailing error in the arrangement of country residences.

Among the contrivances adopted for giving interest to the walks, and to separate one scene from another, are portions of walk covered with arched trellis work. One of these is grown over with climbing roses; another with laburnums, which in the flowering season has a remarkably fine aspect, few colours looking so well in the shade as yellow, because, with the exception of white, none suffer so little from the absence of light. This laburnum trellis has a new feature, that of a table border of trellis work intended to be covered with ivy; we have no doubt its effects will be good, especially in winter.

GOODWOOD; DUKE OF RICHMOND. AUGUST 12. — This is a very extensive place, but without any very striking features, and without water. However, from a belvedere, about half a mile from the house, a very extensive prospect is obtained, which includes the sea and the Isle of Wight. The native woods are very extensive, and chiefly of beech. Miller informs us that one of the Dukes of Richmond planted a great many exotic trees, and especially cedars of Lebanon, and the true service. We saw a good many cedars of a considerable size in the pleasure-ground, and in that part of the park nearest the house; but neither from the kitchen-gardener, nor flower-gardener, nor a man nearly ninety years of age, who had been all his life on the premises, could we learn any thing of the true-service trees.

The great fault of the pleasure-grounds here is, that there is no grand leading walk proceeding from the house through the scenery. Whatever may be the beauties of a residence, they are lost without this master-walk which operates as a leading principle to guide in the emplacement and character of all the details.

We were very much gratified with a view of the house, which we enjoyed unexpectedly, and under very favourable circumstances, it being the week of Goodwood races. The dining-room, drawing-room, and Duchess's room, with the exception of the fire-places and grates, are equal to any thing we ever saw. The dining-room is an oblong, lighted from one side; the walls are painted in imitation of Sienna marble; the furniture, though magnificent, retains still a certain degree of simplicity, which gives the idea of habitableness; the dining-table was laid out to its greatest extent for the visitors during the races; and the row of gilt vases, all won by the Duke's horses at different times, contrasted with the silver and crystal, had a splendid effect.

At one end of the room is the side-board, and at the other the door into the drawing room. This room is apparently the same in shape and size as the dining-room. The end opposite the door from the dining-room terminates in an alcove, the floor of which is raised one or two steps; and in the angle to the right is the door to the Duchess's cabinet, and to the left a door to the hall and staircase. The walls are hung with yellow satin, striped; and the

GOODWOOD – 'THIS IS A VERY EXTENSIVE PLACE, BUT WITHOUT ANY VERY STRIKING FEATURES.'

curtains and sofas, &c. are of the same material, and the wood-work and cornices are gilt. The effect of the gold and yellow satin is good. The whole appeared to us, if the expression is allowable, chastely magnificent, habitable, and occupied as it ought to be. The only things we should wish to alter are the grates. There are some good pictures in the other rooms of the house; a charming picure of the amiable Duchess in the Duke's study; a good mummy; landscapes, by Smith of Chichester; a marriage supper, by Paul Veronese, reduced from an original of the same, 13ft. by 8ft., which we bought in Warsaw in 1815 for 9 ducats, and sold in London in 1818, though it had been much damaged by the fire at the custom-house, for 150 guineas.

Haslemere to Arundel. August 14. — The by-roads in this part of the country are very indifferent, which prevents the traveller from having the full enjoyment of scenery which, from its variety and woodiness, is always agreeable, and, from the portions of extreme distance which occasionally intervene, sometimes striking. The entrance of the London road into Arundel is one of the worst town-entrances in Britain, and reminds us of some of the smaller Alpine towns on the Continent. Nothing could be easier than, by a circuitous sweep to the right, to effect an easy and commodious entrance and exit. The present state of things is dangerous, and creates a prejudice against the nobleman who has, or is supposed to have, the power of removing the evil. There are three inns; but the stranger, if he wishes to see Arundel Castle, is recommended to go to the Norfolk Arms, from whence tickets, as if by authority, are issued for seeing the castle. We hate monopolies of every kind, and therefore cannot approve of this seeming preference, though we believe a sight of the castle would not be refused to any person whatever, and at any time, whose appearance did not forbid the hope of his having the usual fee in his pocket. The Norfolk Arms is a good inn, and we were much gratified to find the landlady, Mrs. Flood, much attached to natural history. Notwithstanding the direction of this immense establishment, and the cares of a family of three of four children, she continues to collect every description of insect which she can find, and to hatch the eggs of moths and butterflies, in order to add the perfect insects to her collection. This collection is arranged in glazed frames, which are hung up in different rooms of the house. She is fond of drawing, and has made portraits of several of the prize animals fed in the neighbourhood. On the whole, she is a woman of very superior mind, and, in testimony of our respect for her, we have sent her this Number of the *Gardener's Magazine,* and one or two of the *Magazine of Natural History*.

ARUNDEL CASTLE – 'THE ONLY THING WHICH CAME UP TO OUR EXPECTATION
WAS THE SITUATION OF THE CASTLE.'

ARUNDEL CASTLE; THE DUKE OF NORFOLK. AUGUST 14. — This is an excellent place for a critic, since there is much to condemn, something to admire, and a great deal to anticipate. The only thing which came up to our expectation was the situation of the castle, and the only thing that surpassed it was the variety of surface and facilities for improvements in the grounds. In the elevation of the castle there is not a single good architectural feature, and we should not be far wrong in saying, that the interior did not contain a single room worthy of such a residence. The library, which has been much spoken of, is too narrow and confined, and the mahogany book-cases, like the mahogany four-post beds in the bed-rooms, overloaded with workmanship. The dining-room is gloomy, and is only fit for the winter season: some of the bed-rooms are better, and contain mahogany bedsteads most elaborately worked; but no workmanship in timber can come up to that of the needle or the loom for a bed roof.

What has been done in landscape gardening is not better than what has been done in architecture. The place is frittered into details, without connection, and without any pervading principle. There are three or four kitchen-gardens, and three of four places that may be called flower-gardens, but not one grand leading walk to show either these or any thing else.

In our excitement at the want of plan, however, we must not forget the fine old trees of different kinds about the castle and in the park. The native trees are the beech, the common maple, and about the castle probably the elm, the ash, and the ivy may be added.

ARUNDEL CASTLE – 'THERE ARE SOME GOOD TREES AND SHRUBS IN A VERY
THRIVING STATE.'

There are many very fine old maples, some curious-rooted elms on the castle banks, some large oaks, and some of the largest ivy we ever saw.

ARUNDEL TO DORKING. AUGUST 16. — An agreeable road through a varied and fertile country. Cnicus acaulis is abundant on the Downs, and the summits of the broad purple flowers, spread out on a level with the surface of the grass, have a fine appearance. At Pulborough a cottage covered with a very large and handsome parsley-leafed grape, which we were told ripened its fruit in ordinary years. In the churchyard four children of one birth in one grave. Some picturesque, Gothic cottage villas on the right of the road, on the margin of a common two or three miles before entering Dorking, most agreeable to look at; but knowing the small, gloomy, low-ceiled rooms which architects generally form in these buildings, as being characteristic of the style, we have no pleasure in the idea of inhabiting them.

The entrance into Dorking is highly enriched by cottages, villas, gardens, trees and hills; the town, as compared with many others may be described as elegant and picturesque. William Fuller, a tinman, makes a very ingenious seed-box for feeding pheasants; and Mr. Carter, potter, makes handsome garden vases, in use at Deepdene and other places.

DEEPDENE; THOMAS HOPE, ESQ. AUGUST 17. — This is a place which presents but little food for the critic, since it contains so much beauty, both by Nature and by art, that there is little left for him to do but walk round and admire. Even the historical associations of the place are beautiful. The situation was distinguished by its natural beauties and delightful prospect so long ago as the time of Charles I, at which time it was selected as the retirement of the Honourable Charles Howard, a man of science and taste, who effected several garden

DEEPDENE – 'NO ONE CAN DULY APPRECIATE ITS BEAUTIES WHOSE MIND IS NOT THOROUGHLY IMBUED WITH ITALY AND THE FINE ARTS.'

DEEPDENE.

improvements here in the terraced style of his time. In Camden's *Britannia,* Deepdene is said to contain "gardens, vineyards, grots, terraces, and plantations." Aubrey, in his *Antiquities of Surrey,* describes it as "a long hope, i.e. according to Virgil *deductus vallis* (a lengthened valley), contrived in the most pleasant and delightful solitude for house, gardens, orchards, boscages," &c. which he had seen in England. Mr. Hope has greatly enlarged the house and offices, and having combined in them all the finest parts of what may be called the landscape architecture and sculpture of Italy, has formed a whole, the greatest praise that we can bestow on which is to say, that it will delight such men as Sir Uvedale Price and Gilbert Laing Meason. The house, with the conservatory and sculpture galleries on one hand, and the dairy, laundry, &c. on the other, forms a group so rich in classic forms and combinations, that no one can duly appreciate its beauties, whose mind is not thoroughly imbued with Italy and the fine arts. It is, in short, an example of what the Germans call the ecstatic in architecture. There is not one English architect who would of his own accord have designed such a house; nor, if he had designed it, could he have found more country gentlemen by whom it would have been understood or carried into execution, than the *Gardener's Magazine* would find readers if it were published in Greek. Accordingly, as we are informed in the account of Deepdene published in Neal's *Views of English Country Seats,* "the house was altered under Mr. Hope's direction, and from his own designs, in which the more recent discoveries in Grecian and Roman antiquities make a prominent feature, by P. Atkinson, Esq."

The property, we are informed in the same work, "consists of above 400 [acres] of pleasure ground, so judiciously disposed, that a walk admitting a pleasing transition of view,

DEEPDENE – IN THE CONSERVATORY

DEEPDENE – IN THE CONSERVATORY

46

DEEPDENE – IN THE GARDENS

47

DEEPDENE – NEAR THE HOUSE

DEEPDENE – A VIEW OF THE SURREY COUNTRYSIDE

of upwards of 12 [miles] may be undertaken without retracing one step. The surface partakes of the greatest irregularity, and the ground, in general bold, sometimes hangs abruptly over the walks, and at others declines in gentle slopes to the level parts.'' We refer to Mr. Neal's work for a historical and detailed description both of the house and grounds, and merely put down some gardening recollections, and but a few, as the almost incessant rains that fell while we remained at Dorking, prevented us from seeing more than the kitchen-garden, and the immediate vicinity of the house.

In the fruit-garden there is an excellent crop of grapes, in a vinery of Mr. Atkinson's construction, and one of peaches in low Dutch pits, like those of Mr. Labouche, without artificial heat of any kind, by which the fruit comes into use between the forced peaches and those in the open air. In a botanic stove in this garden there are forty-nine species and varieties of Hibiscus, recently raised from imported seeds; only one or two of which have yet come into flower. Francisia Hopeana formerly noticed, is here in great luxuriance and beauty. In the open border is a fine specimen of Mr. Barclay's scarlet thistle, and another thistle 8ft. high, which Mr. Woods, who is an excellent British botanist, considers a new species, and we hope it will be named after him. In a smaller inclosure the American and English cranberry are doing remarkably well in beds of dry peat.

The valley, open and sloping to the south, from which this residence takes its name; besides its architectural and sculptured decorations, pheasantry, fountain, grotto, and some rare antiquities, is richly ornamented with groups of American and other rare shrubs and trees, exotics and annuals; and no situation can be better adopted for half-hardy articles. Salvia chamædryoides, with its deep-blue flowers, has a very fine effect in summer masses. The heliotropiums planted out here are of a very distinct variety, large in their leaves and flowers, and so hardy, that they ripen, seed, and sow themselves. Mr. Woods pointed out to us several plants which had sprung up from this year's seeds. The georginas are remarkably good, and the whole of them were raised in the early part of the season from cuttings, the advantages of which Mr. Woods has promised to point out in a professional communication. There is an excellent collection of tree and dwarf roses; and at few places does the yellow rose bloom so freely as here. The Liquidambar and Magnolia tripetala are rising in the woods from self-sown seeds; the former is so abundant that is might pass as indigenous.

The conservatory is highly ornamental from the style of its architecture, the free growth of the plants, the fine disposition of the climbers, the exterior approach through a terraced garden of orange trees and exotics, and above all, its connection with the galleries and cabinets of the most exquisite sculpture, antique and modern. In front of the conservatory is a plantation of orange trees in pots sunk in the ground; and of different descriptions of green-house plants, chiefly from the Cape of Good Hope and New Holland, turned out of the pots into the soil, in order to grow and flower freely during the mild season, and take their chance of standing the winter. The effect in summer is excellent, and it has been found that several New Holland species, such as Acacia dealbata, and others, have survived several winters. We have repeatedly recommended this practice, both with hot-house and green-house plants, not only for the sake of the rare and splendid appearance produced during summer, but for the chance of finding some of the species hardy enough to stand the winter, and thus adding to to our acclimated trees. Every gardener who has a green-house or a hot-house, or even pits, which will keep plants during winter better than either, ought to have a clump on his lawn expressly devoted to this purpose; and in this clump, every May, he ought to turn out all his spare plants. If he has no lawn, he undoubtedly will have borders; and he will find no way of rendering them so interesting as by the use of his spare exotics, especially the free-flowering Cape and Australian plants. Gentlemen's gardeners in the country, who have abundance of showy green-house things, such as pelargoniums, fuchsias, brugmansias, heliotropes, cinerarias, celsias, &c., might give some of them to the cottagers on their masters' estates, for the sake of ornamenting the roadside gardens. Snakes and adders are occasionally seen in the grounds here; but Mr. Woods has nearly extirpated them, by giving 3d. for each of the former, and 6d. for the latter, to his men.

The only fault that we can find with Deepdene is, a want of high keeping in the grounds near the house, and in the fruit and kitchen gardens. We do not speak of the walks in the woods; these, and almost every thing a furlong from the house, are just as they ought to be: the whole place, indeed, may be called well kept; but it does not display that high and polished neatness which the architecture of the house, and its sculptured and classic appendages, seem to demand. The grass about the house ought to be mown oftener, and a part of the walks and road, especially in the focus of art and ornament, laid with Kensington gravel. The walks in the kitchen and fruit gardens, being rather steep, we would form of flagstones, placed on piers, with open joints, by which means they would at all times be in perfect order; whereas now, in consequence of the slope and sandy soil, every shower deranges them. We are sure such walks, at such a place as Deepdene, will be found cheaper in the long run than those of gravel with box edges. These walks formed, and the addition we should suppose of three garden labourers, would make all the difference between Deepdene as it is now, and as it is in our *beau ideal* of what it ought to be.

We do not speak of the sculpture gallery, because, greatly as we admire its contents, and respect the high and cultivated mind that selected and placed them there, we feel that we are incompetent to do it justice. Duly to appreciate works of art of such extraordinary rarity and excellence as are here assembled, would require more of the mind of the artist and the classical scholar than we can pretend to. All must feel the effect of sculptures and paintings to a certain extent; but this feeling, like every other, to be made the most of, must be highly cultivated. The feeling which these sculptures excite in us, when viewing them, is that of reverence and awe at the presence of so much mind; on leaving them, the idea presents itself of the man who has shown his appreciation of such excellence, and we think of him with profound respect. To say a word in the praise of either, we do not think necessary.

Mr. Woods, who stuffs birds, and has formed a cabinet of the objects of natural history found on the estate, has promised us, at some future time, a general account of Deepdene, with a catalogue of its native productions, animal, vegetable, and mineral, with which, we are sure, our readers will be highly gratified. He is above our praise or reward; but we have, nevertheless, sent him a part of Jardin and Selby's *Ornithology*.

THE DENBIGHS – 'THIS HOUSE IS ON TOP OF A HILL, WHICH COMMANDS A FINE PROSPECT.'

DENBIGHS. — This house is on the top of a hill, which commands a fine prospect, with the town of Dorking at its base; and beyond that, Deepdene. The approach is a mile and a quarter in length; great part of it through a plantation, mixed with spruce firs, which, notwithstanding the dry calcareous soil, in 1827 made shoots from 2 to 4ft. in length. This is the more remarkable, since the natural soil of the spruce fir is soft and moist, as in the north of Prussia, and in the Black Forest on the Rhine.

EPSOM NURSERY; MESSRS. YOUNG. AUGUST 18. — This nursery has undergone considerable changes since we last saw it in 1827. At that time it had been enlarged and improved, and one of the foremen, a self-taught draftsman, had made us a general view of it as seen from the road. Since that sketch was made, several plant-houses and pits have been erected, and the most extensive collection of herbaceous plants, at least in Britain, has been assembled.

Messrs. Young have bought the entire stock of Magnolia Soulangiana from M. Soulange Bodin for 500 guineas, in consequence of which that fine tree will soon be spread over the country. The collection of phloxes here amounts to 60 species and varieties, and of Dianthus to 40 species, one of which, the D. Fishceri, is highly odoriferous. A new hardy evergreen honeysuckle was pointed out to us, which, from its rapid growth, promises to be as valuable an addition to our ligneous twiners, as Eccremocarpus scaber is to our herbaceous climbers. Hardy orchideous plants are grown to an extraordinary degree of perfection. In small square enclosures, which they call sanctums and paradises, are many new things not to be shown to the uninitiated till they come into flower, and not to be sold till a number of plants have been propagated. In conclusion, we have to express our highest approbation of the liberality of Messrs. Young, whose collection is at all times open to gardeners and botanists of every description.

In consequence of the continued rains, a good deal of anxiety was very naturally expressed respecting the getting in of the harvest, and, as is usual, different plans have been suggested for drying corn in wet weather. There can be no doubt that the simplest mode of gaining knowledge on the subject of harvesting in a wet season, is to study the practice which prevails in countries or districts wetter or colder than our own. Notwithstanding the very unfavourable weather, and disappointments at Dorking and various other places, we have not passed these fifteen days without instruction and gratification.

EPSOM NURSERY – 'ONE OF THE FOREMEN, A SELF-TAUGHT DRAUGHTSMAN,
HAD MADE US A VIEW OF IT AS SEEN FROM THE ROAD.'

2

A TOUR FROM

LONDON

TO

MANCHESTER, CHESTER,

LIVERPOOL

AND

THE LAKE DISTRICT

MAY – JULY 1831

WITH A VISIT TO
HOOLE HOUSE

We left Bayswater April 24.

The variety of indigenous plants, as seen from the road, in all this tract of country is much less than imagined; partly because a ditch and hedge form a sort of artificial habitat, which has a tendency, wherever it occurs, to encourage the same plants.

Stellaria graminea is found almost every mile, with the exception of some parts of the Peak, from Bayswater to Manchester. The common trees on the London clay are oaks and elms; beech abounds in masses on the chalk; ash on the red sandstone, especially on the drier and richer soils; the wych elm is found on the shady side of limestone hills in Derbyshire and Staffordshire; on the dry parts of such hills, and especially in Dove Dale, the Pyrus Aria abounds; and, in the moister parts, the yew.

We shall say little respecting native birds and insects; the singing birds everywhere were of the thrush family, and of the lark and the linnet kind: in the milder parts, as far as Kidderminster, the nightingale was heard; the plover and cornrail were also heard near Kidderminster. House sparrows, like the house fly and cabbage butterfly, were found everywhere near human habitations.

The weather from the 24th of April to this 24th of June has been chiefly dry; and, until the last three weeks, the wind has been in the east. About the 7th of May a severe frost injured the blossoms and young shoots of both native and foreign plants and trees, over the whole tract included in our tour. The American shrubs were the most severely hurt; their young shoots and their expanded blossom buds being entirely cut off. Even the incipient shoots of the ash tree were blackened, and hundreds of acres of larch and spruce firs in the extensive plantations round Heath House, Alton Towers, Illam, and other places, were

STOWE – 'APPEARS TO US THE MOST PERFECT OF RESIDENCES.'

STOWE

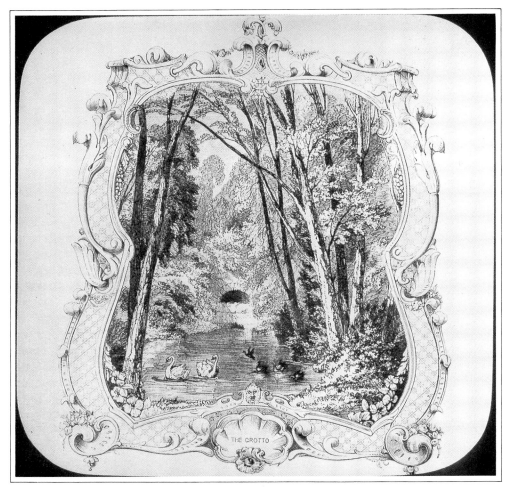

THE GROTTO

STOWE

rendered quite brown, and still continue so. The Scotch pine had not commenced growing, and therefore escaped. Seedlings of every kind in the market-gardens, and in private gardens even the wall trees, have all suffered in a degree only equalled by two or three seasons within the remembrance of the oldest gardeners. The only similar injury sustained in our remembrance was in the spring of 1819. The potatoes in the fields were cut down by the frost; but they have since sprung up again, and their appearance, together with that of the corn crops, is now generally promising.

Having thus slightly indicated the mode of generalising the natural history part of a gardening tour, we shall next attempt to generalise the gardening information obtained.

56

WARWICK CASTLE

Stowe, taking it altogether, and considering it as a work of art, appears to us the most perfect of residences; nature has done little or nothing; man a great deal, and time has improved his labours. The extensive pleasure-grounds have been greatly improved since we first saw them in 1806, by the present gardener, Mr. Brown, who may justly be said to have received the mantle of his great namesake and predecessor in the same garden, our common father in landscape-gardening. We were sorry to learn that these gardens are not kept up as they used to be; the number of hands being yearly lessened. In new and rare plants, trees, and shrubs, the grounds are not keeping pace with the nurseries, as the furniture of the house, especially the grates of the fireplaces, is falling behind the best fashions of the day.

WARWICK CASTLE, has little to recommend it but the house, and the view from its windows. The approach road cut through solid rock, with sides as formal and perpendicular as a drift-way to a mine, or the sides of a canal, still remains in all its deformity, and confirmed the bad impression which it had made on us twenty-five years ago. The pleasure-grounds are worse kept up than at Stowe; and the opaque-roofed green-house, containing the celebrated Warwick vase, is disfigured by sickly pelargoniums, and other commonplace plants. Such green-houses, if they are to have plants in them at all, ought first to have glass roofs; and secondly, only very large plants in large pots or boxes. In such houses no small plant can ever thrive. In the whole world of gardening there is not a sight more disagreeable to us, than that of great numbers of sickly little plants in pots.

WARWICK CASTLE, THE WARWICK VASE IN ITS NEW HOME BUILT NOT LONG
AFTER LOUDON'S VISIT.

ALTON TOWERS is a very singular place, both in its geology, which is peculiarly adapted for grand and picturesque effects, and in what has been done to it by the late Earl of Shrewsbury. The house, or abbey, stands on a piece of table land, of 50 or 60 acres in extent; and this table land is bounded on three sides by two valleys, which commence in a gentle hollow near the abbey, and lose themselves in a third broad and deep valley in an opposite direction,. The surrounding country is composed of similar valleys, among portions of table land or hills. The surface of both hills and valleys is generally in pasture, with very few human dwellings, or in plantations of pines, and large firs, from ten to thirty years' growth. The rock is every where red sandstone, often protruding from the sides of the valleys in immense stratified masses, the exposed parts occasionally worn by the weather into anomalous shapes, but at a little depth under ground affording excellent stone for building. The natural character of this

ALTON TOWERS – 'WHAT MAY BE SAID TO HAVE ECLIPSED, AND STILL TO
ECLIPSE, EVERYTHING ELSE (IS) A VALLEY, NATURALLY IN A HIGH DEGREE
ROMANTIC WITH WOOD, WATER AND ROCKS, FILLED WITH WORKS OF THE
HIGHEST DEGREE OF ART IN ARCHITECTURE AND GARDENING.'

part of the country is grand and picturesque, with a solitary and wild air, approaching to the savage.

The remains of a very old castle, belonging to the Shrewsbury family, exist on a rock protruding into one of these valleys; but the site of the present abbey was, twenty years ago, nothing more than a farm house. Here the late Earl of Shrewsbury commenced his operations, and employed hundreds of labourers, mechanics, and artisans, from 1814 till his death in 1827.

This nobleman, abounding in wealth, always fond of architecture and gardening, but with much more fancy than sound judgement seems to have wished to produce something different from everything else. Though he consulted almost every artist, ourselves among the rest, he seems only to have done so for the purpose of avoiding whatever an

ALTON TOWERS – 'ONE OF THE MOST SINGULAR ANOMALIES TO BE MET WITH
AMONG THE COUNTRY RESIDENCES OF ENGLAND.'

artist might recommend. After passing in review before him a great number of ideas, that which he adopted was always different from every thing that had been proposed to him. His own ideas, or his variations of a plan that he had procured, were transferred to paper by an artist, or clerk of the works, whom he kept on purpose; and often, as we have been informed by Mr. Lunn, the late gardener, were marked out on the grounds with his own hands. The result, speaking of Alton as it was at the time of the late earl's death in 1827, and as we saw it shortly before, viz. in October, 1826, was one of the most singular anomalies to be met with among the country residences of England. An immense pile of building in the way of house, with a magnificent conservatory and chapel, but with scarcely a habitable room; a lofty prospect tower, not built on the highest part of the grounds; a bridge and an embankment over a valley, without water underneath; ponds and lakes on the tops of hills; a quadrangular pile of stabling in the midst of the pleasure ground; and, what may be said to have eclipsed, and still to eclipse, every thing else, a valley, naturally in a high degree romantic with wood, water, and rocks, filled with works of the highest degree of art in architecture and gardening. The private approach roads to Alton, on every side, are several miles in length; they are conducted along the bottoms and sides of winding rocky valleys, with a stream in the bottom, and the sides more or less wooded. It is difficult to decide whether the best approach be that from Uttoxeter or that from Cheadle. We arrived from the former town in 1826, and from the latter this year.

By the road leading from Uttoxeter we came unexpectedly close to the house, and near the head of the north side of the valley, which contains the chief wonders of the place. The first objects that met our eye were the dry Gothic bridge and embankment leading to it, with a huge imitation of Stonehenge beyond, and a pond above the level of the bridge alongside of it, backed by a mass of castellated stabling. Farther along the side of the valley, to the right of the bridge, is a range of architectural conservatories, with seven elegant glass domes, richly gilt. Farther on still, to the right, and placed on a high and bold naked rock, is a lofty Gothic tower or temple, consisting of several tiers of balconies round a central staircase and rooms; the exterior ornaments numerous, and resplendent with gilding. Near the base of the rock is a fountain, of a peculiar construction, which is amply supplied from an adjoining pond. Behind, above, and beyond the range of conservatories, is a lake, and, beyond the lake, another conservatory with curious wings and statues; below the main range of conservatories are a paved terrace walk with a Grecian temple at one end, and a second terrace containing a second range of conservatories. The remainder of the valley, to the bottom and on the opposite side, displays such a labyrinth of terraces, curious architectural walls, trellis-work arbours, vases, statues, stairs, pavements, gravel and grass walks, ornamental buildings, bridges, porticoes, temples, pagodas, gates, iron railings, parterres, jets, ponds, streams, seats, fountains, caves, flower baskets, waterfalls, rocks, cottages, trees, shrubs, beds of flowers, ivied walls, rock-work, shell-work, root-work, moss houses, old trunks of trees, entire dead trees, &c., that it is utterly impossible for words to give any idea of the effect. There is one stair of 100 steps; a cottage for a blind harper, as large as a farm house; an imitation cottage roof, formed by sticking dormer windows, accompanied by patches of heath to imitate thatch, and two chimneys, on a large mass of solid rock, which, seen at a distance, on a steep bank embosomed in wood, bore naturally some resemblance to the sloping roof of a cottage grey with lichens.

As the sandstone rock protrudes from the sides of the valley in immense masses, abundance of use has been made of it to form caves, caverns, and covered seats; it has even been carved into figures, and we have Indian temples excavated in it, covered with hieroglyphics, and in one place a projecting rock is formed into a huge serpent, with a spear-shaped iron tongue and glass eyes. There is a rustic prospect tower over an Indian temple, cut out of solid rock on the highest point of the north bank; and, in the lowest part of the valley, there are the foundation and two stories (executed before the death of the late earl) of an octagon pagoda, which is to be 100ft. high, and to spout water from the mouths of 100 dragons. This pagoda, the Gothic temple, the range of gilt conservatories, and the imitation

ALTON TOWERS – 'A COTTAGE FOR A BLIND HARPER, AS LARGE AS A FARM HOUSE.'

of Stonehenge, of all which we have been furnished with elevations, form the leading artificial features of the valley. The valley itself is upwards of a mile in length; it gradually widens from its commencement at the stone bridge with the pond above it, till it terminates by opening into a very wide valley, containing a considerable stream and a navigable canal. This last immense valley, it is said, the late earl intended to cover entirely with water; and, as it would have saved the Canal Company a mile or two of canal, they offered to form the dam or head at their own expense.

In approaching from Cheadle, we arrive in front of the castellated stables, and see

ALTON T

ALTON TOWERS – 'A HUGE IMITATION OF STONEHENGE.'

the abbey across the pond above the level of the bridge. Proceeding a little farther towards the dry bridge, Stonehenge appears in the foreground, and the seven gilt glass domes of the main range of conservatories below. Raising the eyes, the lofty Gothic temple appears on the left of the picture; and on the right, across the valley, the harper's cottage. In the centre of the picture, over the domes in the foreground, the valley loses itself in a winding bank of wood, in a style of great grandeur and seclusion. None of the details of the valley here obtrude themselves; and the stranger, coming from a wild country with no marks of refinement, on this view so unexpectedly, must feel it to be singularly impressive. It strikes him with surprise, and fills him with astonishment and delight, to find so much of the magnificence of art amidst so much of the wildness and grandeur of nature. The imitation of Stonehenge, too, is a feature in artificial landscape which we have not elsewhere seen, and a stranger is puzzled and confounded by finding a stream and a small waterfall, supplying a lake on what he conceives to be the highest point of high ground.

Thus far as to the first impressions. We shall not here go into details. It is evident that the contents of the valley defy all criticism; and that, perhaps, is paying the author a compliment after his own heart. If his object were originality, and that of a kind which

ALTON TOWERS – 'A RANGE OF ARCHITECTURAL CONSERVATORIES, WITH SEVEN
ELEGANT GLASS DOMES, RICHLY GILT.'

ALTON STATION

ALTON TOWER

ALTON TOWERS – THE COLONNADE

IN STAFFORDSHIRE

ALTON TOWERS, VIEWS OF THE GROUNDS

ALTON TOWERS, VIEWS OF THE GROUNDS

ALTON TOWERS, VIEWS OF THE GROUNDS

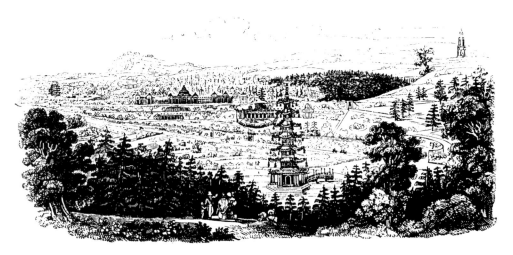

ALTON TOWERS – 'AN OCTAGON PAGODA, WHICH IS SAID TO BE 100FT. HIGH AND
TO SPOUT WATER FROM THE MOUTHS OF 100 DRAGONS.'

should puzzle and confound, he has certainly succeeded; and having attained the end which he proposed, as far as it respects himself, he is to be considered a successful artist. How far it may be commendable for a man of wealth to gratify a peculiar taste, rather than one which is generally approved by the intelligence of the country in which he lives, is not in these days, perhaps, a question of much consequence.

It gives us pleasure to observe that the valley is kept in excellent order by Mr. Miller, a reading and scientific gardener. For this purpose, a number of women are constantly employed in weeding, sweeping, picking up dead leaves and insects, cutting off decayed flowers, and tying up straggling shoots, &c.; a practice which we cannot but highly commend. On certain occasions, these women are put into Swiss dresses, which must add to the singularity of effect. The plants in the conservatories are in their utmost beauty, chiefly through frequent removal. The conservatory at the house, with its plants, trays of choice flowers, sculptures, candelabras, vases of alabaster, stained glass windows at the extreme ends, chandeliers with coloured burners, exotic birds in magnificent cages, &c., surpasses any thing of the the kind we have ever seen, and forms a suitable approach to the splendidly furnished gallery into which it opens.

CHATSWORTH has always appeared to us an unsatisfactory place. The house is not situated on a platform of adequate size; and there is great awkwardness in the approach proceeding abruptly up hill. A square pile of building, too, in such a situation, is less suitable than a lengthened one; and the waterworks, though good in themselves, are scattered about the grounds in such a way, that, while they interfere everywhere with the natural beauties of the place, they no where combine in forming one grand artificial effect. They want concentration. The improvements now going on will probably remedy most of these evils. The house is being extended in length; there is an opportunity of concentrating the waterworks in the only situation fit for them, on the west front; and the approach may be made by a bridge across the river, directly on this front, to arrive at the house on a level. All, or almost all, the artificial waterworks we would form on this west front; and, instead of the cascade of twenty-four steps on the east front, we would lower the earth, and carry from the house a level surface diminishing in width back to the base of the rock lately laid bare by Mr. Paxton, and so produce a waterfall from a precipice of upwards of a hundred feet in height.

The kitchen-garden here contains twelve acres, and, as the foreman informed us, there are twenty-two men allowed for keeping it in order. With regard to weeds, it was cleaned down to the economic point; but the box- edgings were ragged; and, in one part, a long bed of ornamental plants was introduced, and bordered by turf serrated on the edges, or, as the ladies call it, vandyked. Nothing of this sort ought, in our opinion, ever to be introduced in such a kitchen-garden as that at Chatsworth; we would as soon introduce a plot of cabbages in the newly formed parterre at the house.

We regret that we did not find Mr. Paxton at home; and this circumstance prevents

CHATSWORTH – 'THE HOUSE IS NOT SITUATED ON A PLATFORM OF ADEQUATE SIZE.'

us from saying more on the subject at present. All the neighbouring gardeners agree in stating that he has greatly improved the garden department at Chatsworth, and we are happy in adding our testimony to the same effect.

It is most gratifying to us to be able to state that the Duke of Devonshire allows all persons whatever to see Chatsworth, the house as well as the grounds, every day in the year, Sundays not excepted, from ten in the morning till five (the latest hour at which the house can be entered) in the afternoon. The humblest individual is not only shown the whole, but the duke has expressly ordered the waterworks to be played for every one, without exception. This is acting in the true spirit of great wealth and enlightened liberality; let us add, also, in the spirit of wisdom.

MANSION RESIDENCES. — Too great an extent of pleasure-ground, for the number of hands allowed to keep it in order, is an error that prevails everywhere. We scarcely know an exception; and the consequence is, that we have hardly seen one mansion residence kept in the order to which it ought to be.

Most proprietors of mansions have, within these few years, been obliged to curtail the number of hands allowed to their gardener; and, under such circumstances, the plan we should recommend would be, to reduce and concentrate the highly kept part of the pleasure grounds, and keep it near the house; never to attempt higher keeping at a distance from the house than is to be found at it, and leave all distant parts to run comparatively wild, but keeping the walks in good order, though without trimming their edges, or digging or hoeing the the surface among shrubs.

It is very common among places of this class to have flower-gardens, or perhaps a green-house and parterre of flowers, at some distance from the house, with a portion of commonplace shrubbery, lawn, and gravel walk intervening. We conceive this to be in very bad taste. To whatever extent avowed art is carried, the highest degree ought almost to be nearest to the most avowedly artificial object, viz. the house; and, from the garden front of that, art ought to spread along the lawn and the walks, diminishing in proportion to the distance, till it loses itself in scenery comparatively natural. Were this principle properly understood and acted upon, the money now spent upon even those places where the hands are greatly reduced, would produce tenfold the present effect. It would, in fact, give satisfaction; whereas, miles of walks and acres of land, in a state of mediocrity, never can give pleasure to the gardener or the stranger visitor, and surely not to the proprietor.

VILLA RESIDENCES. — The faults of the villa residences which we have seen are, to a certain extent, those of the mansion residences; and there are other faults, both in the original laying out and in the keeping and management, which are also common to both. We shall pass over the ridiculous twisting and turning of walks, without real or apparent reason, which is so frequently met with, and rather dwell on the bad shapes and improper places of groups of shrubs and flowers on lawns. In several parts of this Magazine we have laid down the fundamental principles which ought to guide the placing of groups, viz. to arrange them so as to render them cooperating parts, with those which surround them, in the formation of one whole. It is not very easy to convey this principle to a mind that has not been a good deal cultivated in respect to the beauty of lines and forms; or to a person who has not had some practice in sketching landscape.

It can be no disparagement to gardeners, to affirm that there is not one of them in a hundred who has acquired the sort of knowledge requisite for the purpose of planting what are called single trees. For this purpose, a painter's eye is indispensable; and a gardener may be at the very head of his profession as a horticulturist, a florist, and an arboriculturist, and be, in addition, an excellent botanist, and yet be altogether without a painter's eye.

Though we are not a professional architect, yet we pretend to as thorough a knowledge of the principles of architecture, as of those of landscape-gardening; and, though the architects who design buildings to our taste are not quite so few as the gardeners who lay out grounds to please us, yet by far the greater number of them are as completely without the painter's eye as are the generality of gardeners. The greater number of even the best architects are the slaves of rules drawn from precedents instead of from principles; and this, indeed, is the great bar to improvement in almost every thing. The fundamental principles of architecture are of two kinds, because its objects are two, viz. use and beauty: fitness, strength, and durability compose the first of these principles; the idea of an expressive whole, the second; and in an extended sense of the word, this principle will include the other. A whole in architecture, as in landscape-gardening, may be regularly symmetrical, or irregularly symmetrical. In the one case, as in the other, the test of success is the production of a whole expressive of the purpose for which it is intended.

It would occupy too much space, to go into the faults of architectural details; prevailing ones in every description of edifice are, the use of detached columns as ornaments, instead of component parts; the employment of half and three quarter columns as component parts of walls; and the placing of pediments where they cannot, by any possibility, be the ends of roofs. Tried by these tests, how few buildings are there that will not be found wanting? But this must be the case till architects become not only mechanical contrivers but artists and philosophers. To know what is perfection in any art, it must be tried by metaphysical principles.

TOWN GARDENS. — Under this denomination we include the gardens and grounds attached to houses in streets, and also the gardens belonging to persons living in towns, but which are detached from their houses; the latter being gardens of culture only.

The detached town gardens are situated in the suburbs of towns, generally collected together, and separated by hedges. There are upwards of two thousand of such gardens in the neighbourhood of Birmingham, a considerable number at Wolverhampton, some at Dudley and at Manchester, and a few even in the neighbourhood of that stationary town Buckingham.

It is not uncommon for single men, amateurs, clerks, journeymen, &c. to possess such gardens, and to pass a part of their evenings in their culture. In one of these gardens, occupied by Mr. Clarke, chemist and druggist, Birmingham (the inventor of *Clarke's Marking Ink*), we found a selection of hardy shrubs and plants which quite astonished us.

COTTAGE GARDENS. — By these we understand the gardens attached to cottages in villages, or to the humbler class of dwellings scattered through the country. In the agricultural district from London towards Warwick they are small and poorly cultivated, in comparison with those around Birmingham and the other manufacturing towns. The cause is too obvious to require explanation. We are not sure, however, that the culture of flowering shrubs against the walls of cottages is so general in the manufacturing as in the agricultural districts. We expected greater progress to have been made among the gardens of the miners in Derbyshire, where we found, indeed, in Middleton Dale, and at Castleton, some cottages without gardens. We recommend this subject to the Duke of Devonshire's agents, and to Mr. Paxton, who might distribute plants and seeds among them.

We left Manchester on July 1. The lake district, besides its adaptation for the growth of timber and for pasture, is, by its varied surface, rocks, and waters, admirably suited for the summer residences of persons engaged in business in towns; and as soon as railroads are completed between London and the large manufacturing towns of the north, including Lancaster and Carlisle, an event which must inevitably take place before ten years have elapsed, we hope to see the hills thickly studded with villas and cottages from their bases to their summits. This seems to us the second step in the progress of the application of the lake scenery to the purposes of human use and enjoyment, as covering it with pasturage and wood was the first, and as the establishment of water-mills will be the third. We are aware how much this prospective view will shock a number of the present residents on the lakes; but we cannot sympathise with exclusiveness, even in natural scenery. Nature made the lakes and the surrounding rocks and mountains in all their rudeness, as she made the crab and the sloe: from these man has produced the golden pippin and the green-gage plum; and why should not the same spirit of improvement be directed towards those parts of Cumberland and Westmoreland which, relatively to man, are as wild as the crab or the sloe? All objects and things ought to be judged of with reference to the whole of human nature, and not with reference only to some particular part of it.

The weather during July has been remarkably warm, with frequent showers; and on the whole the agricultural crops and woods never looked better. The crops of fruit, however, are generally defective, though we believe they are better in the neighbourhood of Manchester and Chester than they are either farther north or farther south. On the 15th of July a dreadful hailstorm happened at Penruddock, about six miles from Penrith, on the road between that town and Keswick. It extended over a tract of country nearly two miles in diameter, totally destroying the field crops, and killing many of the birds, hares, rabbits, and poultry. The hares took shelter in the same shed with men and cattle. The leaves of the large Tussilago, by the roadside, and those of all the crops in the cottage gardens were cut into shreds; the potato leaves and stems were lacerated, and every stalk of corn was broken. Two extensive farmers lost every thing but their cattle. The storm began in darkness, about four o'clock in the afternoon, and continued nearly two hours; the hailstones which fell were from 4 to 6in. round; they formed a body in many places from 15 to 18in. deep; and lay on the ground three days before they were all melted.

Elevation, moisture, and temperature have much more influence on native vegetation than soil. The unity of the flora of the roadsides the whole way from London to Dumfries is beautifully preserved by the bramble and the common polypodiums. These last are very numerous in the neighbourhood of Birmingham, on the coarse sand; and equally so among the lakes between Newby Bridge and Keswick, on the soft compact clay. In shady situations, for example, about Levens, near Milnthorpe, and on the east side of Windermere, where the road passes Storr's, the Polypodium vulgare has established itself on the trunks and branches of even healthy vigorous-growing trees, in a manner quite remarkable, and which reminds us of the descriptions given by travellers of the epiphytes in the forests of Demerara and South America. Some sycamores and limes, by the side of the public road at Levens, have their trunks and branches thickly covered with long black moss, in which this fern flourishes most luxuriantly; and a fine oak in the garden of the poet Wordsworth, at Rhydal Mount, is similarly clothed, though not to the same extent. In the drier districts of England this polypodium confines itself to the decaying trunks of old pollards. The wild strawberry is very common on old banks on the sandstone, and also on the clay, and it has grown and spread so vigorously in the neighbourhood of Bowness, and on the banks of the Esk between Longtown and Langholme, as to form on the stone fences strawberry walls. Other walls at Levens, and among the lakes, are completely covered with ferns, which spring from every joint, and from the turf coping.

VILLAGES. An individual of taste, and of an amiable disposition, who happens to be placed in a village, may, even in the present very imperfect state of things, do much in the way of ornamenting and improving it. We have seen a fine instance of this in the village of Bowness on Windermere. Mrs. Starkey, who has ornamented her own house and ground, situated in that village, with many of the finest plants and shrubs, offers seeds of young plants freely to every villager who will plant and take care of them. Mr. Starkey has purchased some ground and widened the village street where it was narrow, devoting a marginal space to evergreens and flowers, unprotected by any fence. Mrs. Starkey has also planted and carefully trained laurels, box, and holly, against the churchyard wall. In other situations, where laurels would not grow, she has planted ivy; some chimney tops she has ornamented with creepers, and others she has rendered more picturesque by architectural additions. Mrs. Starkey's own house, which is entered directly from the village street, is ornamented by a veranda which extends its whole length. Independently of woody climbers of the finest sorts, which remain on this veranda all the year, pelargoniums, georginas, maurandias, lophospermums, and other similar plants, are planted at the base of the trellised supports, and flower there during the summer. At the opposite side of the street is another piece of trellis-work, as the fence to a flower garden: this trellis, when we saw it, was partially covered with purple and white clematis, sweet peas, nasturtium, calampelis, pelargoniums, and georginas. These hung over into the street in profusion; and the gardener assured us that no person, not even a child, ever touched a flower or a leaf. Mr. Starkey (a Manchester manufacturer) had not yet arrived there for the season, and the house was in consequence shut up; but of this circumstance the villagers took no advantage. In the gardens of this village, and in part also in those of Ambleside and Grasmere, may be seen many of the new potentillas, geums, lupines, clarkia, &c.; and against the walls, kerria, Cydonia japonica, China roses of different sorts, clematis, and other climbers are not uncommon. The village of Bowness affords a proof that, when the public are treated with confidence, they will act well in return; and that, notwithstanding what has been said of the rudeness of John Bull, he will, when treated like the French and Germans, become as considerate and polite as they are. It it true, the working inhabitants of London and of manufacturing towns cannot be expected all at once to pay the same respect to flowers as the inhabitants of Bowness; but time will remedy this evil.

OF PALACE RESIDENCES we have, since our last, seen only two; Eaton Hall and Lowther Castle. The palace at Eaton Hall, in the exterior, equalled our expectations, and in the interior surpassed them. It is the only palace which we have ever seen where every part of the finishing and furniture was equally excellent, and all in perfect harmony and keeping. With great splendour, there is great chasteness of colouring; and, in consequence, an appearance of comfort and habitableness that one does not expect to meet with under such a gorgeous exterior. Having said this, and added that the kitchen-garden is in perfect order and keeping; its character being that of a kitchen-garden, ornamented with flower-borders, we have said all that we can say in favour of Eaton Hall. As to the grounds; in the first place, the situation forbids all hope of any natural beauty in the park, beyond that of the grouping of trees, and the excellence of the pasture and roads; and in the next place, a totally wrong character has been attempted in laying out the pleasure-grounds about the house. A dreary even surface, every inch of which is seen from the terrace, has been attempted to be varied by three broad parallel walks, and one cross walk, with beds along their margins.

We were rather surprised to find this pleasure-ground in very bad order; the white clover was flowering on the grass; on remarking which to an intelligent young man, Mr. Duff's foreman, he stated that the grass was keeping for the farmer, that article being scarce with him this season. This, the family being in London, we consider to a certain extent a legitimate excuse; but we wonder much that a man of the Earl of Grosvenor's rank and wealth, possessing such a truly magnificent palace as Eaton Hall, should not give orders to have it, at all seasons, in the highest style of keeping of which it is susceptible.

EATON HALL – 'THE PALACE AT EATON HALL, IN THE EXTERIOR, EQUALLED OUR
EXPECTATIONS, AND IN THE INTERIOR SURPASSED THEM.'

EATON HALL – 'WE WERE RATHER SURPRISED TO FIND THIS PLEASURE GROUND
IN VERY BAD ORDER.'

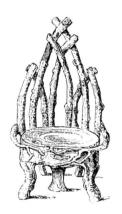

TATTON PARK

MANSION RESIDENCES. The house at Tatton Park is finely situated; but the park, though naturally much varied, and containing a fine piece of water seen in the middle of the picture from the garden front, has too many single trees. It is injured, because by this means a sameness of appearance is produced, and there is everywhere a thin sprinkling of trees, instead of broad masses of wood and lawn, broken at their margins, and entering into each other. In short, what landscape-painters call breadth of feature is wanting.

VILLA RESIDENCES. We have found a few of these very perfect; viz. Hoole House, Lady Broughton's; the villa of Mr. Barber, at Grasmere; Mrs. Starkey's villa, at Bowness; the poet Wordsworth's, at Rhydal; and the garden of Mr. Tong's cottage, near Garstang. We regret the want of room to describe these places. Mrs. Starkey's villa, at Bowness, is perfection's self, as far as it goes; for, though the area of the grounds is not much larger than that of the magnificent library at Eaton Hall, they contain more beauty and variety than the whole of the hundred acres of pleasure-grounds at that great dull place. Rhydal Mount is a pastoral cottage, many of the walks being of turf. There is a terrace walk, with some scraps of natural rockwork planted by art; and displaying at the same time the taste of the painter in the arrangement of the colours, and the science of the botanist in choosing the plants. Mr. Tong's flower-garden, at Falcon Cottage, is formed in the bottom and on the sides of an old gravel pit or quarry; and is one of the most successful productions of the kind that we have ever seen. The first object that met our eye in the foreground was a cone, 10 or 12ft. in diameter, and 6 or 8ft. high, of Potentilla formosa; and the next, high up in the rocky bank, a

RHYDAL MOUNT – 'A PASTORAL COTTAGE, MANY OF THE WALKS BEING TURF.'

mass, covering several square yards, of the dwarf white Campanula. To the right and left were masses of beautiful and rare flowers in blossom. The gate was ajar, though there was no person belonging to the garden in it; for here there is no dread of the public; and we walked in, sending a message to Mr. Tong. In threading our way through the intricacies of this enchanted garden, we found it planted with shrubs and plants for spring and autumn in such a manner as render it gay all the year. Every new and rare plant which has been recommended in this Magazine is to be found here; and, what is most remarkable of all, Mr. Tong, who is chiefly his own gardener, and a good botanist, told us, that, three years ago, he knew only about half a dozen of the commonest flowers.

A Return Visit to Hoole House

Hoole House, the Rev. Peploe W. Hamilton; occupied by Lady Broughton.

Hoole is a residence situated about two miles from the city of Chester, on the road to Liverpool.

We saw Hoole in 1831, and were exceedingly desirous of giving some account of it in our tour published at that time in the *Gardener's Magazine;* but, as it is strictly a private residence, and not shown to any person whatever without permission, except to the friends of Lady Broughton, we could not then prevail on Her Ladyship to accede to our wishes. Having in January last seen at Mr. Lonsdale, the eminent artist's, some exquisitely beautiful water-colour drawings of the flower-garden and rock-fence at Hoole, we could not resist the temptation of renewing our application to Lady Broughton, for permission to take engravings of them for publication. To this Her Ladyship very reluctantly consented, being

HOOLE HOUSE – 'A RESIDENCE SITUATED ABOUT TWO MILES FROM THE CITY OF CHESTER.'

unwilling to give publicity to her place; but, having consented, she permitted us to employ a land-surveyor to take a general plan of the garden. We have now, therefore, to express our sincere thanks to Lady Broughton for acceding to our request, and for enabling us to gratify our readers with some account of the flower-garden at Hoole; and, while we do this, we feel it right to express our anxious hope that the additional publicity which we are now giving to this unique place may not induce any one to endeavour to break through a rule rendered necessary to the comfort of Lady Broughton, in consequence of the living-rooms being close upon the garden and opening into it.

The surface of the ground at Hoole is flat, and the soil a rich loam. In the extreme distance, in one direction, are seen the Welsh mountains, in another, the Peckforton Hills and Beeston Castle.

HOOLE HOUSE, THE GROUNDS.

The striking effect produced by the flower-garden at Hoole depends on the contrast between the smooth flat surface of the lawn, with the uniformity of the circular beds, and the great irregularity of the surrounding rockwork. The length of the flower-garden, within the rocky boundary, is 60 yards, and the breadth 34 yards.

The design of the rockwork was taken from a small model representing the mountains of Savoy, with the valley of Chamouni: it has been the work of many years to complete it, the difficulty being to make it stand against the weather. Rain washed away the soil, and frost swelled the stones: several times the main wall failed from the weight put upon it. The walls and the foundation are built of the red sandstone of the country; and the other materials have been collected from various quarters, chiefly from Wales; but it is now so generally covered with creeping and alpine plants, that it all mingles together in one mass. The outline, however, is carefully preserved; and the part of the model that represents "la Mer de Glace" is worked with grey limestone, quartz, and spar. It has no cells for plants: the spaces are filled up with broken fragments of white marble, to look like snow; and the spar is intended for the glacier. We may add that it is equally impossible to create anything like it by mere mechanical means. There must be the eye of the artist presiding over every step; and that artist must not only have formed an idea of the previous effect of the whole in his own mind, but must be capable of judging of every part of the work as it advances, with reference to that whole. In the case of this rockwork, Lady Broughton was her own artist; and the work which she has produced evinces the most exquisite taste for this description of scenery. It is true it must have occupied great part of her time for six or eight years past; but the occupation must have been interesting, and the result, as it now stands, must give Her Ladyship the highest satisfaction.

The rockwork is planted with a selection of the most rare and beautiful alpines, particularly with all the close-growing kinds; each placed in a nidus of suitable soil, and the surface protected from the weather by broken fragments of stone, clean-washed river gravel, the debris of decaying rock, moss, or other suitable substances; according as the object was to retain moisture; to evaporate moisture, in order to prevent the plants from damping off; to increase the heat, in which case dark fragments of stone are used; or to diminish it, which is effected by the employment of white pebbles, which, by reflecting the light and heat, keep the ground cool.

Pl. 76.

Garden Varieties of Pelargonium
1. Large flowered White 2. Gem 3. Sunrise 4. Ariat.

PELARGONIUMS, FROM MRS. LOUDON

G. Pickering

OCKERY

ARAUCARIA IMBRICATA AT DROPMORE

3

A TOUR IN

MIDDLESEX, BERKSHIRE, BUCKINGHAMSHIRE, OXFORDSHIRE, WILTSHIRE, DORSETSHIRE AND HAMPSHIRE

JULY – SEPTEMBER 1833

The last time we passed deliberately through this tract of country was in 1812 and 1813; and, comparing it as it is now with what it was then, we have been much gratified by some things, and found cause for regret at several others. We have found a decided improvement in the cottage gardens, we may say everywhere, by the more frequent appearance of flowers in them, and by the prevalence of the China rose, trained against the walls. The cottage dwellings are, on the whole, not worse; and on some estates they are a good deal improved. Many cottages, which before had no gardens, have now considerable portions of ground added to them; unfortunately, not generally adjoining the cottage, but in some neighbouring field; but still there is now hardly a cottage which has not ground attached to it in some way or other.

Plantations of trees have been made in many places which were unenclosed common when we last passed through them; and by the formation of these plantations, and the increased growth of others, the general aspect of the landscape is, in many parts of the country, entirely changed. We were nowhere more struck with this than on the road between Oxford and Woodstock, which, instead of the bleak and dreary appearance it formerly had, is now bordered with belts of trees, and sprinkled with cottages. There are now on this road no less than three nursery gardens.

The roads have been everywhere more or less improved, but still they fall far short of what they ought to be.

With respect to gardens and country-seats, we may say, that, on the whole, we never saw them in a state of worse keeping. Generally speaking, the more extensive the park and gardens, the worse they are kept. We scarcely recollect above one or two noblemen's places highly kept; and even one of these will no longer be an exception to the general rule, since pecuniary difficulties have occasioned eleven garden labourers to be discharged from it at once. The noblest place in Britain, perhaps in Europe, Blenheim, is going rapidly to decay. Almost the only highly kept gardens which we saw were those of small proprietors, professional men, merchants, or bankers.

MRS LAWRENCE'S VILLA, VIEWS IN THE GARDENS

Among the larger places of the greatest natural beauty, and judicious general arrangement, were Highclere, the Grange, and Broadlands. We never were more struck with any thing than with Highclere, particularly with the variation of the grounds and views, and with the disposition of the trees. The first sight of the portico at the Grange, looking down upon it embosomed in wood, from the grove on the opposite bank, came upon us like enchantment. But, lest we be thought partial, or should forget some person or place that ought to be mentioned in these rather hurried introductory remarks, we shall now proceed to details; premising that the whole of the remaining portion of these notes was written, ready for the press, while on our tour, every evening or the following morning; so that the remarks on each place form an exact transcript of what we felt at the time of seeing it.

MRS. LAWRENCE'S VILLA, DRAYTON GREEN. —JULY 27. This place, of limited extent, and possessing no material advantage except that of a dry soil on a subsoil of gravel, has been rendered a perfect *bijou* of floricultural beauty by the exertions and taste of Mrs. Lawrence. All the most rare and beautiful hardy flowers and peat earth shrubs are here assembled, and beautifully disposed in groups, in the natural or picturesque manner, on the smoothest lawn; interspersed with a few trees, and decorated with fountains, statuary, vases, rockwork, and

MRS LAWRENCE'S VILLA, VIEWS IN THE GARDENS

basketwork. There is a green-house full of choice articles; and there is not a plant that is not grown in the very highest degree of perfection, or a scene that is not in the highest order and keeping. Among the plants that struck us as profusely covered with bloom, and beautifully grown, were the single and double Clematis florida, the yellow Chinese and yellow Noisette roses, the Calandrinia grandiflora, Petunia phœnicia and nyctaginiflora, all the new fuchsias, showy nicotianas, Lupinus mutabilis, and others.

A straight line or row of shrubs, used as a screen, is successfully varied by acute triangular projections on the turf, in the manner of what mantua-makers call vandykes (in allusion to the style of shirt-collar usually found in Vandyke's portraits); the triangles are of irregular size, at different distances of from 3ft. to 5ft., and are filled with flowers. The lawn here is one of the most beautifully kept we ever saw; and it is shaven with the mowing machine alone, with only the assistance of shears at the roots of the shrubs. Mrs. Lawrence attributes much of the high order and keeping of the whole to the care and attention of her head gardener, Mr. Cornelius, brother to the foreman of that name in the hot-houses of Messrs. Lee's nursery.

MRS LAWRENCE'S VILLA, DRAYTON GREEN – 'THIS PLACE ... HAS BEEN RENDERED
A PERFECT *BIJOU* OF FLORICULTURAL BEAUTY BY THE EXERTIONS AND TASTE
OF MRS LAWRENCE.'

MRS LAWRENCE'S VILLA, VIEWS IN THE GARDENS

STOKE PARK – 'THIS IS A VERY INTERESTING PLACE ON MANY ACCOUNTS. ITS
PRESENT POSSESSOR IS THE GRANDSON OF THE CELEBRATED PENN, THE
FOUNDER OF THE STATE OF PENNSYLVANIA.'

STOKE PARK, J. PENN, ESQ. — This is a very interesting place on many accounts. Its present possessor is the grandson of the celebrated Penn, the founder of the state of Pennsylvania; and, had this gentleman's father not been a royalist, his income from his American possessions, we are informed, on the best authority, would now have exceeded six hundred thousand pounds a year. Stoke Park is also interesting, as being the scene of Gray's *Long Story,* and of his celebrated *Elegy in a Country Churchyard.* The yew trees immortalised by the poet are still in existence; but most of the "rugged elms" have been cut down. What we principally regretted, however, was the removal of nearly all the old Elizabethan mansion, which is said to have been one of great architectural beauty. Gray was buried in the churchyard; and near it, in the grounds, there is a plain massive pedestal, surmounted by a sarcophagus, erected to his memory. On the four sides of the pedestal are four appropriate extracts from his *Elegy.* There is also a monumental column in the park, to the memory of Sir Edward Coke, the celebrated lawyer. The grounds consist of a considerable extent of table land, from which an irregular winding slope descends to the south. This slope is very gentle; but it is still sufficient to give the walks along the brow, and especially the house, command-ing views of Windsor Castle and the adjoining country. The grounds were first modernised under the direction of Mr. Repton, about the time when he and Mr. Main were laying out those of Chalfont House; but they have been since almost entirely changed by Mr. Penn, and his present most intelligent gardener and land steward, Mr. Osborne. The pleasure-ground is laid out in what may be called the classical style of the poet Mason; the forms of the masses of flowers and shrubs being generally circular or oval, and each scene distinguished by

94

appropriate statues, or busts on therms, like those formerly in the flower-garden at Newnham Courtney. The house in the Grecian style, and Doric, appears to a stranger remarkably well placed, though, like most others built about the same time, it wants an architectural basement and appendages. The summit is crowned with a cupola, which, from want of showing deep reveals to the openings, has a temporary air, as though it were built of boards, and coloured in imitation of stone. The truth is, it was an after-thought, and these are always bad.

DROPMORE, EARL GRENVILLE. —JULY 31. Beautiful as this place always is, it has been very much improved since we last visited it in 1826.

A new entrance lodge has been formed on the Burnham side, covered with trunks of trees, in the manner of a Russian log-house, with a chimney top in the style of those of Venice; rather an incongruous assemblage, which forms a false note of preparation for a place which, in other respects, is generally in consistent taste.

The flower-garden at Dropmore shows what may be done by art on a surface wholly without natural advantages. The effect is produced by the arrangement of the beds, and by the distribution of pedestals with vases, statues, and other sculptures, and by therms and other mural and architectural ornaments. To connect the whole with the house, there is an architectural wall, with an open Italian parapet in the front of its border in one place, and in others various hot-houses, which are placed against it. The vases and sculptures are partly of real, partly of artificial stone, and partly of china-ware. There are benches with carved backs, made of wood, but painted and sanded in imitation of Bath stone, which are particularly good; as are a number of fountains, candelabra, and other ornaments; as well as a manner of

DROPMORE – 'BEAUTIFUL AS THIS PLACE ALWAYS IS, IT HAS BEEN VERY MUCH IMPROVED SINCE WE LAST VISITED IT IN 1826.'

forming pedestals of open brickwork for supporting scultures. The parapets are of artificial stone, or brickwork covered with cement; the wall against which the hot-houses are placed is of brick, covered with trelliswork; and the hot-houses are of wood, painted green. This green colour in the hot-houses and the trellises is what we can never reconcile ourselves to: it detracts from the avowedly artificial character of the rest of the scenery. In walking through the grounds, we were everywhere, as in 1826, charmed and delighted; and we were still more so now than then, at finding the number of rustic stands, vases, &c. diminished. The pinetum has received numerous additional species, and the sorts which were rare in 1826 have now attained a considerable size, and some have been found hardier than expected. We

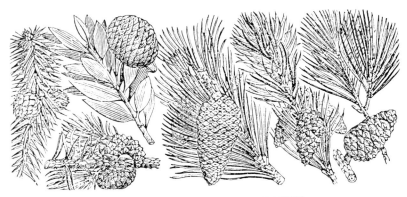

DROPMORE, VARIOUS PINES IN THE GROUNDS.

particularly allude to Cunninghamia lanceolata and Araucaria imbricata, both of which are found so hardy as to stand here without protection.

It is almost needless to state that in the flower-garden were to be found all the new, rare, and beautiful hardy flowering plants. We were particularly struck with the number of plants of that gorgeous iridean bulb, Gladiolus natalensis (psittacinus), splendidly in bloom; Madia elegans, Petunia phoeœnicea, Calandrinia grandiflora, and Verbena venosa, which produces underground stolones, and is particularly fitted for filling a bed in a very short time. Tournefortia heliotropioides is likewise well adapted for beds, and also Nicotiana longiflora, which we found profusely covered with odoriferous flowers. The day being cloudy, the œnotheras had a splendid appearance.

Mr. Frost is endeavouring to naturalise many plants, both annuals and perennials, in the woods, by planting and sowing there all his spare plants and seeds. It is incredible what may be done in this way, since it has been proved that the seeds of some stove annuals will remain in the open ground during our winters, and come up and flower vigorously during summer.

VIRGINIA WATER. — We saw the whole of this much talked of scene for the first time; and, like most of the other garden scenes of George the Fourth, it entirely disappointed us.

As to architectural ornaments, a gorgeous Chinese fishing-house has been built; having a highly enriched roof with gilt ornaments, set down amidst the common woods of the country, and with nothing exotic around it. In another place, a quantity of the Elgin

VIRGINIA WATER – 'WITH THE CASCADE AND ROCKWORK WE HAVE NO FAULT
TO FIND.'

VIRGINIA WATER – 'A GORGEOUS CHINESE FISHING HOUSE HAS BEEN BUILT.'

VIRGINIA WATER – 'THE GRECIAN FRAGMENTS WHICH ARE PUT TOGETHER WITH
CONSIDERABLE TASTE.'

marbles, consisting chiefly of shafts of columns, with fragments of capitals and architraves
and some Flemish and other statues, have been set down equally without appropriate
scenery; with the exception, however, of an arch, serving as a viaduct for the public road. At
the dam built to raise the lake, a very good cascade has been produced; and in one or two
other places there are some stones arranged in imitation of rockwork. With the cascade and
rockwork we have no fault to find; and little with the Grecian fragments, which are put
together with considerable taste: but all the rest we consider bad.

THE FLOWER-GARDEN AT WINDSOR CASTLE has received the addition of a number of marble
vases, and statues, some of them cast in metal, and some of marble. Some of these are from
the antique, and some in the style of Louis XIV.

In some of the vases there were a few shabby half-starved fuchsias and other green-
house plants, which would be considered a disgrace in a cottager's window; and the few
flowers introduced in the beds were chiefly yellow lupines, marigolds, and other of the
commonest annuals. In the centre there is a fountain, issuing from the orifices of a piece of
metal resembling the rose of a watering-pot. The horizontal jets, which rise only an inch or
two above the water, and extend almost in contact with its surface, have an exceedingly good
effect, by giving great agitation to the water; but there is much want of a perpendicular

central jet. The view from the noble terrace round this garden is, for richness and grandeur, as far as we know, unrivalled.

INN AT SALTHILL. —AUGUST 5. This house, which has attained great celebrity for furnishing all the comforts of private life to the higher classes, has had the character also of a garden inn, to our knowledge, for the last thirty years. The veranda, when we first saw it, was hung with festoons, from one end to the other, of Cobœa scandens; and it is now varied by many of the finest modern creepers. At the foot of the supports, the finer sorts of fuchsias, pelargoniums, calceolarias, and other green-house exotics, are flourishing with as great luxuriance, and as completely untouched by passengers, as if they were bordered by a lawn in front of a gentleman's seat. We can only compare this veranda with that at Mrs. Starkey's cottage at Bowness, similarly circumstanced: a proof, among many that might be adduced, that the public will never injure things meant to be enjoyed by them.

TAPLOW LODGE, MRS. TUNNO. —This is a pleasing place, of considerable extent. A striking feature, in approaching to the entrance front, is a detached conservatory with glass on all sides, and an architectural elevation, by Mr. Robert Stewart of Great Russell Street. The head gardener here, Mr. Holland, who is one of our correspondents, showed us remarkably fine crops of melons and Ribston pippins, the latter apple having this season produced large crops everywhere. A small conical-shaped tree of the Hawthornden apple was so laden with fruit from the base to the summit, that it presented a perfect cone of apples, the stem of the tree being totally concealed, and even great part of the leaves. Mr. Holland grows succory here in the open garden, during the summer season, and, in winter, he plants the roots in boxes, and places them under a stage in a house for forcing flowers, thus producing tender, crisp, and finely flavoured salad throughout the winter. The Cucumis flexuosus, or snake gourd, is here being grown to great perfection as a curiosity.

There is an elegant aviary for canaries, on a board against which are some verses by one of the Misses Tunno, addressing the birds on the subject of their want of liberty, which do equal credit to the head and heart of the authoress.

WINDSOR CASTLE, THE FLOWER GARDEN – 'THE VIEW FROM THE NOBLE TERRACE ROUND THIS GARDEN IS, FOR RICHNESS AND GRANDEUR, AS FAR AS WE KNOW, UNRIVALLED.'

TAPLOW COURT

TAPLOW COURT, EARL OF ORKNEY. — This place is nobly situated; the house, with the pleasure-grounds being placed on the brow of a lofty bank of the Thames, and commanding a noble reach of that river, with an extensive prospect of the fertile and well-wooded country beyond. The ruins of an old church adjoining the house, and a yew tree of very great age on the summit of a mount, form fine objects. The exterior architecture of the house and offices has been begun to be improved in the old English manner. A number of old walls have been pulled down, and the scenery on the lawn thrown open. The effect is excellent. There is a terrace walk here, on the summit of the bank, about 300ft. above the level of the river, nearly two miles in length; which, taken altogether, might be made one of the finest things of the kind in England, and probably in the world.

TAPLOW HOUSE, PASCOE GRENFELL, ESQ. — The house is situated half-way down the same high bank on which is placed Taplow Court, Park Place, Cliefden, Hedsor, and a number of other fine places, commencing at Richmond, and extending, on the same side of the river to near Reading, where the banks become level on both sides. The house is here, very properly, entered from behind; and the view from the principal rooms commands the Thames and Windsor Castle. The grounds are not very extensive; but the lawn slopes most beautifully, and it is judiciously varied by choice trees and shrubs, and beds of flowers, the latter of the rarest and most beautiful kinds, assiduously and successfully cultivated, and kept in the most exquisite order by the gardener, Mr. Springall, who has been in that capacity here for thirty years, and has planted nearly every tree, and laid out every bed. The first view of the lawn front of the house, bosomed as it is in verandas covered with creepers and in banks of flowers, as seen from a dark walk near the lodge, through which strangers are introduced, operates like enchantment. We never were more delighted with anything in a small place. On one end of the house is a beurré d'Aremberg pear tree, 30ft. high, covered with fruit. Turning round before the steps which descend from the drawing-room to the lawn, the latter is varied by beds of flowers which lose themselves among trees, shrubs, and glades in every direction, but so far below the eye, that, when looking at them, the distant scenery is not taken into the landscape. Raising the eye, we catch the Thames and Windsor Castle between the tops of the trees.

Mr. Springall is enthusiastically devoted to his profession, and is in his garden, as he informed us, from four o'clock in the morning till it is dark at night. His master never interferes with his management, and this will always be found to be the case, when the garden is so well conducted as it is here. Mr. Springall lives in a pretty thatched cottage by the road side, with an octagon front, and a veranda ornamented by creepers; he has also a very neat flower-garden in front. Opposite the entrance to Taplow House is another handsome cottage, with a beautiful flower-garden in front, evidently under the superintending care of Mr. Springall; so that the general impression, both on entering and leaving the place, is that of comfort, neatness, and fine flowers.

Park Place, [-] Maitland, Esq. — We walked over the whole of the ruins, as they may be called, of this once magnificent place, in company with the excellent and very intelligent gardener, Mr. White; and often did we think of what it must have been in the time of the Prince de Ligne, when he went over it with its then proprietor, General Conway. At that

PARK PLACE – 'IT IS GRIEVOUS TO SEE GENERAL CONWAY'S BUILDINGS ALL
GOING TO DECAY, WITH THE SINGLE EXCEPTION OF THE DRUIDICAL TEMPLE
PRESENTED TO HIM BY THE INHABITANTS OF THE ISLAND OF JERSEY, WHERE HE
WAS SOME TIME GOVERNOR.'

time between forty and fifty men were employed in keeping it in order, and now there are only three, with one woman, kept for the same purpose. To expect any thing like high keeping, therefore, is quite out of the question, though it is really wonderful how much Mr. White has been able to effect with means so circumscribed. We cannot help deeply regretting that such a place is not kept up as it ought to be. It is grievous to see General Conway's buildings all going to decay, with the single exception of the druidical temple presented to him by the inhabitants of the island of Jersey, where he was some time governor; and the rustic bridge, over which the public road is carried, and under which there is a vista of the Thames. Near the house are some magnificent old trees, particularly a cedar planted by George III., and supposed to be the most stately cedar tree in England, which we doubt not may be the case: if any surpass it, it must be some of those at Whitton.

The Thames, as seen from the Druid's temple, contains an island, which, with the banks and the general outline of both the island and the river, might afford an excellent lesson to landscape-gardeners in imitating tame rivers in level parks. Park Place has long been celebrated for its lavender plantations, which occupy between 40 and 50 acres. The plants are raised from cuttings, which are slipped off and prepared by women in the autumn, and bedded in, in rows, in any spare piece of garden ground, where they remain for two years. For three of four years a row of turnips or potatoes is grown between the lavender; after which period, or about the time that the lavender plants in the row touch each other, half of them are removed, leaving the field covered with plants 4ft. apart every way. In a few years the plants touch each other; and in this state they will remain from 15 to 20 years, according to the nature of the soil: they are then taken up, and the ground cropped for two or three years with turnips and other field crops; after which the lavender plantation is renewed. The flowers are obliged to be either sold to a regular licensed distiller, or distilled on the premises, on account of the excise laws. The oil from the plantation here is said to be of the best quality; doubtless, from the calcareous nature of the soil.

LAVENDER COTTAGE, — [-] GRAHAM, ESQ., is finely situated on a knoll, backed by the woods of Park Place, and having the Thames at a short distance from the boundary of its lawn, the public road on the right, and the lavender plantation stretching away to the left along the base of the chalk hills. In General Conway's time, this was the house of his steward; but it is now let as a gentleman's residence.

THE MARKET OF READING is well supplied with the commoner vegetables and fruits, and particularly with apples and cherries. The latter fruit this year is very abundant, and of excellent quality. The cherry market is held on Wednesdays and Saturdays, and on the last market-day, the 7th inst., the price was 1s. 6d. per score pounds. The last cherry market for the season will be held on Saturday. It is a pity that the cherry-growers have not learned the art of making kirsch-wasser. Flowers, both cut and in pots, are brought to market on Saturdays, both from market-gardens and private gardens.

Great quantities of green-house plants in pots have been exposed for sale in the market-place, from the gardens of private gentlemen, and also hawked round the town in carts.

THE GARDEN OF THE READING GAOL well deserves notice in a work, the great object of which is to promote a taste for this art. It is, as may be supposed, small; but the governor has a taste not only for gardening, but for natural history. He has, on his lawn or grass plot, a beautiful piece of rockwork, composed of flints and fragments of mural antiquities. He has, also, a variety of plants of the choicest kinds, such as Wistaria, double furze, Ribes several species, Petunia phœnicea, and numerous pelargoniums, the whole mixed with fruit trees. Every advantage was taken of the high brick walls of the gaol for training vines and fruit trees. The governor had also a collection of fancy rabbits, a beautiful cockatoo, &c. The prisoners were watering the plants; and we can only account for the neatness of the whole from the abundance of hands at the command of the master. On looking through the prison we felt, as we did at Aylesbury, in 1831, the deepest regret at seeing so many persons imprisoned for mere trifles, without any reference to their reformation; which imprisonment, as the gaoler himself remarked, could only have the effect of making them worse.

AUGUST 7. In proceeding along the Newbury road to Englefield House, we observed, on the left, the circular reservoir of cast iron, which supplies great part of the town of Reading with water. It is about 50ft. in diameter, and about 12ft. high (we speak from a casual view), and is placed on a base of brickwork about 3ft. high. If the latter had been higher and more architectural, and if the upper part of the cast-iron rim had been also architectural, and the surrounding fences removed, so as to leave this structure in an open area, it would have formed a noble public ornament.

In crossing the country to Strathfieldsaye, we observed a remarkably large yew tree in the churchyard at Sulhampstead. At Mortimer Street, the vicarage house has a very beautiful flower-garden and shrubbery, with a piece of water, the beauty of which may be fully enjoyed by passengers on the road. The grounds consist of two banks of turf, which slope down to the pond, and the whole is considerably below the eye of a person walking along the road. It would be easy to shut it out by a hedge of ordinary height, but we recommend the taste and good feeling of the proprietor, in wishing his neighbours and the public to participate in his enjoyments. We know nothing of this vicar, not even his name; but we have little doubt that he is a good man. It seems to us that every man, in ornamenting his house, his garden, or his estate, however small it may be, ought to consider not only his own gratification, but the ornament and benefit of his country. He ought always to ask himself, what the passers by will think of what he is doing.

STRATHFIELDSAYE, HIS GRACE THE DUKE OF WELLINGTON. — We entered this noble park by an avenue a mile in length of elms, of a broader-leaved kind than the common English elm, and forming a tree of less altitude. The surface over which this avenue passes is undulating, which detracts somewhat from its first impression; but, as it is found to increase in length as we advance along, the sentiment of grandeur is recalled, and by prolongation is even heightened. We expected the surface of the grounds to be flat, but were agreeably surprised to find a gentle hollow running through them in the direction of the length of the park, in the bottom of which hollow is the river Loddon, widened, and otherwise heightened in effect. The park is as well wooded as could be desired, with trees of all ages and sizes, but chiefly with old oaks and elms. The avenue of elms terminates at a short distance from the house, where the pleasure-ground commences on the left, and a plantation continues to the kitchen-garden and stable offices to the right.

We met Mr. Cooper, the very polite and well-informed gardener, at the com-

STRATHFIELD SAYE – 'WE ENTERED THIS NOBLE PARK BY AN AVENUE A MILE IN
LENGTH OF ELMS...'

mencement of the pleasure-grounds, and walked round them and the kitchen-garden with
him, leaving the place afterwards by the London approach, which branches from the avenue
in a winding direction at about two thirds of its length from the house. The pleasure-ground
is of very limited extent, and perfectly flat; but it contains some very fine specimens of cedars,
larches, Weymouth pines, spruce firs and other foreign trees.

Mr. Cooper forces 25 sorts of figs; the duke, like ourselves, esteeming that fruit
beyond all others. Some trees which Mr. Cooper has removed from a wall to a forcing-
house are 45 years old. There is a vinery stocked with plants 6 years old, producing an
excellent crop. Mr. Cooper has invented a very excellent utensil for sending cut flowers to
London, or to any distance, without injury: It is simply a cylinder of tin, or of any other
suitable material, of 3 or 4 feet in length, and 8 or 9 inches in diameter. In the centre of this is a
cylinder of tin of an inch in diameter, which fits into sockets in the bottom and in the lid.
Round this small cylinder the flowers are tied as they are upon a maypole; the pole so charged
is inserted in the socket in the bottom, then the tube is filled with water, and corked, and the
lid put on, in which is a socket, which embraces the tube. The case may now be sent to any
distance, the water keeping the flowers cool and fresh. Mr. Cooper informed us that the
Duke of Wellington gave him some chestnuts which he had received from America,
gathered from the tree which General Washington planted with his own hands, and from
which (more fortunate than we have been, though we have received chestnuts three times
from the same tree, once from Mrs. Seaton of Washington, and twice from Dr. Mease of
Philadelphia,) he has raised three or four plants. We should be curious to know on what
principle these chestnuts were sent to the Duke of Wellington; not that the merits of the latter
general are at all less than those of the former, because we believe that the actions of all men
are the joint results of their organisation and the circumstances in which they are placed; but
that we should like to know the feelings of the sender, and whether he was a Briton or an
American. We have always had a great respect for the straight-forward character of the Duke
of Wellington, and a profound admiration of General Washington; but with reference to all

104

1 Gladiolus Namaquensis. 2 Gladiolus Natalensis. 3 Gladiolus trichonemifolius.
4 Gladiolus Algoensis. — 5 Gladiolus Colvilii. — 6 Gladiolus Watsonius. —

Day & Haghe Lith. To the Queen.

GLADIOLI, FROM MRS. LOUDON

PICEA NOBILIS AT DROPMORE

Pl. 45

1 Nicotiana tabacum. 2 Nicotiana acuminata. 3 Nicotiana noctiflora. 4 Nicotiana multivalvis
5 Nicotiana longiflora. 6 Nicotiana glutinosa. 7 Nicotiana persica. 8 Nicotiana Langsdorfii.

NICOTIANAS, FROM MRS. LOUDON

Pl. 27

1 *Fuchsia macrantha*   2 *Fuchsia serratifolia*
3 *Fuchsia splendens*   4 *Fuchsia radicans*

FUCHSIAS, FROM MRS. LOUDON

that is essentially grand in human nature, we have never for a moment placed the former on a par with the latter. As to the Duke of Wellington's private character as a husband and a master, all that we have heard at Strathfieldsaye and its neighbourhood places him, and also the late duchess, very high in our estimation. A spot was pointed out to us where it was intended to erect the new palace, the model for which, we were informed, is in one of the rooms of the present house. We hope it is not a frigid compilation in the Grecian or Roman manner. We should wish to see a magnificent pile in the old English or Italian style.

The charger which the duke rode at Waterloo is kept in a paddock adjoining a small flower-garden, from which the late duchess used frequently to feed him with bread from her own hands. During the battle, the duke was on this horse 15 hours, without once dismounting, and it has never been ridden since that day. It is a small chestnut horse, slightly made, and, as it was quite a colt at the time of the battle, it is wonderful how its strength was equal to the excessive fatigue it must have undergone. There is a proverb in some parts of England, that a chestnut horse is always a good one, and that it will always do more work than any horse of the same size, of any other colour, and this horse seems to furnish an illustration of its truth.

BEAR WOOD, JOHN WALTERS, ESQ. M.P. — Being in this neighbourhood in 1818, we had an opportunity of walking over these grounds shortly after they were purchased by the present owner. They then appeared to consist of about 300 acres of heathy waste, and about 100 acres of sloping ground covered with beech and oak trees. A small piece of water was forming on the side of the slope; the walls of the kitchen-garden were built, and the site of the intended house was pointed out to us. The place may not be considered as finished; and we must say, that it has afforded us more gratification than any other newly formed place that we have seen since we left London.

A considerable portion of the grounds is preserved in their original wild state, covered with heath and dwarf furze; and this part, being passed through previously to arriving at the dressed grounds near the house, has an excellent effect.

We by no means dislike the elevations of the house at Bear Wood, which may be characterised as a cottage villa. There are a handsome porch for driving under on the entrance front; and a semicircular colonnade of coupled square columns in the centre of the garden front, with an elegant balcony over. Joined to this is a large conservatory, forming a bend, in Mr. Nash's manner, and serving as a passage to a billiard-room; but in consequence of the roof of this conservatory being very high, and darkened with the foliage of vines, the plants below do not thrive, and the intention of this elegant appendage is in a great measure defeated. On the entrance front of the house there are rather too many walks and rides, parallel to each other, seen at once: but this may be easily remedied, even if the house be retained in its present situation; and entirely avoided, if it should be removed.

We recommend Bear Wood both to the wealthy citizen who wishes to create a country residence, and to the young gardener who is desirous of acquiring the art of laying out grounds. To the former we recommend it, as showing the sort of soil, which, from its general unsuitableness for corn culture, as well as from its dryness and its elevated situation, may most economically and judiciously be employed in plantations and pleasure-grounds, and as a healthy site for a house.

At Bear Wood, the young gardener will learn more of landscape-gardening than in any other place which we know, within the same distance of London. He will there see a practical illustration of the principles of massing, grouping, and of every kind of planting; of varying the outline of water; of managing pieces of water on different levels; and of judiciously thinning plantations.

CAVERSHAM PARK. —AUGUST 9. We proceeded to this place through the village of Caversham (in which are many beautiful cottage gardens), up the hill road, and entered by the back approach. We must notice one of the cottage gardens, which has, in two angles, formed by small wings projecting from the front of the house, two small green-houses in the form of outside cupboards, with shelves full of pots of flowers, the glass doors being removed. We had never seen anything of this kind before, and we like it, not that we think it in good taste, but because it shows such a thorough love of plants. Every one who has read the descriptions of the fine old places of England, in Whately's *Observations, &c.,* knows something of Caversham, and therefore we shall say nothing of the magnificent mansion, containing fifty rooms, and its broad gravelled terrace, 50ft. wide and a furlong in length, on a perfect level. Though the mansion is dilapidated within, yet exteriorly it is in good repair. The place is worth visiting for the grandeur and beauty of the situation of the house, the terrace, and more especially the descending approach, which has been so finely described by Whately. The pleasure-ground scenery is now entirely overgrown, and only to be recognised by a few cedars and other trees. The kitchen-garden forms a deplorable ruin; the walls are overgrown with bushes, the hot-houses leaning in all directions, the back sheds roofless, and even the gardener's house, which held out till within these few years, uninhabitable. The commanding position of the mansion, and the extensive and varied prospect seen from it, are the same as they ever have been. Among the trees along the descending approach are a number of very large maples.

Comparing Caversham Park with Bear Wood, the situation of the house, in the former case, is very much more commanding than in the latter, because of its greater elevation. The prospect is also more extensive for the same reason, and because the base of Caversham Park is the broad and extensive valley of the Thames.

There is thus an essential difference between these two situations; for, though both are grand, but in different degrees, yet, in one, the grounds are positively varied and beautiful, while those of the other are wholly without either beauty or variety. For a constant residence, it is evident that the place containing the greatest natural variety and beauty would be by far the more desirable, independently altogether of the heightening of these beauties by gardening.

The ride from Reading to Pangbourne, along the banks of the Thames is one of very great beauty. The valley is about half a mile in width, bounded on each side by chalk hills, exhibiting the greatest variety of outline; sometimes clothed with grass, and at other times with corn or wood, or crowned by a gentleman's seat. Near Purley is Purley Hall, a place of considerable beauty, from the undulation of its surface, and the judicious disposition of its woods. There are also some beautiful cottages with gardens, and some small villas, both at Purley and Pangbourne.

BASILDON PARK, SIR FRANCIS SYKES, BART. — The house, a large quadrangular pile with wings, by Carr of York, is placed on a piece of table land on the top of a hill, and commands very extensive views. The ascent to it is by a very steep approach, which is both disagreeable and dangerous. We repeat here, what we have frequently stated before, that in no possible case need the road to a house be steeper than an inch to a yard. The approach here might have been led to the house at that rate with the greatest ease, and horses might have trotted up and trotted down. There is but very little pleasure-ground, and this is placed on one side of the house; but the park and farm are of considerable extent. The pleasure-ground has been taken care of for many years past by a local labourer, of the name of Hillsbury, who appears to have some natural taste for laying out flower-beds. He showed us different scroll-like shapes which he had laid out, and lamented his ignorance of the names of plants and their culture. His master, he said, had ordered him to collect some "fir apples" (cones), and sow the seeds of them, and he would be glad to know the proper season for doing so, with the manner of sowing, &c. This shows the great necessity of gardeners being reading men, and possessing books on the subject of their art. This man is doubtless an honest and faithful servant, as he has held his present situation, as he told us, nearly 30 years. We observed also a paling fence round a part of the pleasure-ground, with the pales, instead of being placed vertically, nailed to the rails at an angle of 45 degrees. The object of this, we were told, is to prevent the entrance of rabbits, which might get between upright pales at the same distance apart, but which must necessarily place their bodies in an angular position to get through these. This, it is found from experience, they cannot readily do.

BASILDON PARK

BASILDON PARK, DETAIL OF GATE PIER.

BASILDON PARK, THE GROTTO.

BASILDON PARK, THE VIEW FROM THE RIVER.

MONGEWELL, UVEDALE PRICE, ESQ., NOW OCCUPIED BY MRS. BATHURST. — Our principal object, in visiting this place, was to see if there were any remains of the botany and gardening of the celebrated Daines Barrington; and of the landscape-gardening of Major Price, an amateur, who assisted the late Bishop of Durham in laying out some part of the grounds here, and who laid out Frogmore, and also a small place at East Sheen near Richmond, the residence of Lord Chief Baron Macdonald. We were on the whole disappointed. Nothing remains that can be attributed to Daines Barrington, and there is only a small flower- garden, which, we were informed, was laid out by Major Price. It is an irregular glade, partly surrounded by trees, but open to the south, with a walk round it, and the turf varied by roundish clumps. Altogether, it is very well designed, and it is kept very neatly.

The church is close by the house, and near the latter are a flower-garden and an opaque-roofed green-house. The plants were out, and their place was supplied by a large table and several chairs; on the table were bulbs, that the young ladies, we were informed, were sorting, naming, and putting away in bags for the planting season; thus occupying themselves at once usefully and agreeably. Close by the kitchen-garden we met with Mr. Munn, a native of Bedfordshire, who has been here 47 years; part of the time as gardener, and the remainder as steward and general manager of the estate. He is a fine elderly gentleman-like man; and, when we saw him, it being evening, he had on his blue apron, with his watering-pot in his hand for watering his own garden, and seemed to us a personified *beau ideal* of a gardener of the old school, such as we may see in some of the frontispieces to the works of Mawe or Abercrombie. He is very intelligent, and, among other interesting things, informed us that a sum of money was left for keeping up for ever the fine old geometric gardens at Wrest Park, Bedfordshire, where he had been gardener in his youth. This sum, he said, was sufficient to pay 14 men throughout the year, and that number would keep the gardens in the highest possible order and neatness.

WALLINGFORD. AUGUST 10. This is a comfortable little town, on the site of a Roman station. The ancient fosse forms three right-angled sides of a square, of which the Thames is the fourth. A few years ago, Wallingford was unknown in the annals of gardening; but of late it has become celebrated for florists, of whom our esteemed correspondent, the Rev. J. Tyso, constitutes the life and soul.

The garden of Mr. Tyso's residence may be considered that of the parsonage-house of the very respectable body (the Baptists) to which he belongs, and it is in part used as a burial-ground. It was something new to us to see peach trees arranged on the walls, and graves and tombstones in the compartments; but on expressing our surprise to the reverend occupier, he replied, that, if this congregation continued to increase as rapidly as it was now doing, the whole of his garden might be occupied in the same manner. We were much gratified to learn, from this gentleman, that though there are a number of varieties of the protestant species of Christianity in Wallingford, yet not only the members but even the clergy of the different congregations all live in perfect harmony. We sincerely hope that the period will soon arrive when all religions and all clergy shall be placed upon a footing of equality in every respect, each depending for support on his hearers; and, when this is the case, we feel certain that Christian harmony will be confirmed in such a manner that neither time nor accident shall be able to prevail against it.

NUNEHAM COURTENAY, A SEAT OF THE ARCHBISHOP OF YORK, is a place which has long been celebrated. We first saw it in 1804, when we visited it in the course of our walking tour. The orangery, and the flower-garden laid out by Mason, were then in great perfection. The roof, front, and two ends of the orangery were movable; and the orange trees, being planted in the soil, when the frame was removed, and the ground turfed over, appeared as if growing in the

NUNEHAM COURTENAY, — 'A SEAT OF THE ARCHBISHOP OF YORK.'

NUNEHAM COURTENAY, — 'THE F

IS MUCH OVERGROWN.'

open lawn. The trees were then in vigorous growth, and covered with flowers and fruit. These trees no longer exist, having been destroyed, partly through the difficulty of heating the house in the winter season; but chiefly, as report states, through the carelessness of the gardener, who succeeded the worthy old man who had charge of them in 1804. The present gardener, Mr. Brodie, informed us that he had seen pieces of the trunks of these trees nearly 1ft. in diameter. The flower-garden is now overgrown with elms and other common trees; the number of the flower-beds is reduced, and the shapes of most of those remaining have been altered. The covered seats are either removed, or in a dilapidated state, and the same may be said of the statues, busts, and therms. Nevertheless, we recognised the scene at once, by the three low arched entrances of a small summer-house. This spot is not longer fit for growing flowers, from its being now too much under the shade of lofty trees. Extensive architectural alterations have been made in and about the house and offices, and improvements in the kitchen-garden have just been commenced, by doing first what is too frequently left to be done.

As it rained fast during the whole of the time we were here, we had little opportunity of examining things in detail. Nevertheless, we saw at a glance that the handsome terrace which has been added in front of the house is badly contrived, with reference to its connection with the pleasure-ground; a proof, in addition to those which we are continually observing, of the necessity of villa architects having a general knowledge of landscape-gardening.

BLENHEIM.—*AUGUST 11.* On the evening of our arrival, we went to the great gates of the approach from Woodstock, and entered, hoping to catch the last rays of the setting sun lingering on the towers of the palace, and to see the deep broad shade thrown on the surface of the lake by the colossal bridge, and the massive oak woods beyond; a spectacle which we had often enjoyed with delight in former times. The view altogether disappointed us; for, looking down on the lake, the surface of which is more than 100ft. below the eye, half of it appeared quite green with aquatic weeds. Next morning we proceeded to the same gates with greater deliberation.

The head, or dam, of the lake is so much out of repair, that it does not retain the water so high as it ought to do by several feet; and the water of the stream, instead of falling over the cascade as it used to do, finds its way under ground, and rises up like springs in the bed of the river and in the flat ground below. The joints of the masonry of the bridge are becoming the nidus of plants, and in a year or two this building alone will produce a tolerable flora. The side entrance, through which strangers are admitted to see the house, is beginning to be dilapidated, and a large portion of stone from the architrave over the gateway has lately splintered off and fallen down.

On entering the grand hall, we were struck by the long vistas through doors to the right and left; and also by the view through two doors to the lawn in front: on turning round, and looking towards the bridge, the long straight avenue passing over it, and having in its centre, at a certain distance, the lofty column crowned by the statue of Queen Anne, completes the impression of dignity and grandeur. This avenue was formerly continued in a straight line for six or eight miles through the Ditchley and Heythrope demesnes, including the mansions of each in the line of the avenue. There is something very grand, and at the

BLENHEIM – 'ON THE EVENING OF OUR ARRIVAL WE....ENTERED, HOPING TO
CATCH THE LAST RAYS OF THE SETTING SUN, LINGERING ON THE TOWERS OF
THE PALACE.'

BLENHEIM – 'THE JOINTS OF THE MASONRY OF THE BRIDGE ARE BECOMING THE
NIDUS OF PLANTS AND IN A YEAR OR TWO THIS BUILDING ALONE WILL
PRODUCE A TOLERABLE FLORA.'

same time very sociable, in the idea of thus connecting three magnificent residences. We see from these straight lines, right angles, and lengthened vistas, how well Vanbrugh understood grandeur of effect, both in architecture and in the principal features of its accompaniments.

After seeing the house, by the permission of the duke we were shown through the private garden. Much has been said respecting this garden, but there is, in truth, nothing remarkable in it; and the duke can only wish it to be kept private, in order to prevent his walks being intruded upon by the numerous visitors, who every day in the year, come to see the house and grounds. Those who have seen Blenheim before this private garden was fenced off, will recollect the bank of lawn, commencing at the library front of the house, and extending to the cascade. They will also recollect the portion beyond the cascade, partly below it, containing some fountains; and partly above it, where there used to be some old mutilated statues. The lawn in front of the library, and these two portions of the grounds, are included in the duke's private garden; the extent of the three scenes being estimated at about 80 acres. There seems no reason why the occupier of such a place as Blenheim should not have a private garden, in the same manner as he has private apartments; but it is surely not allowable that, for this purpose, he should monopolise all that is by nature, as well as by the art which had been exercised before his time, the finest part of the grounds.

Near the house, and from that to the cascade, the surface is sprinkled with choice trees and shrubs, planted in dug patches, in the usual manner. These patches seldom contain more than a single tree or shrub, or a standard rose, with a few flowers round its base. There are at the same time a number of large patches or masses, containing azaleas, rhododendrons, and other flowering shrubs, intermixed with flowers. Some of these masses are bordered by young oaks, twisted so as to form a wreath.

Among the other old trees, besides the oaks, are some deciduous cypresses and Lombardy poplars; but the greater part of both these latter have been cut down since we last saw the grounds in 1810. The poplars were generally considered to be the oldest and finest in England; the few which remain are decayed at the top, and cannot last many years. The deciduous cypresses are also decaying; though large, they are smaller than those at Syon. There is a Portugal laurel, the branches of which are 100 yards round at the base; those of the Portugal laurel in Eastwell Park, in Kent, are considerably larger. A green-house in a tent-like shape has been formed at one angle near the house; and a handsome rustic shed, open on all sides, and covered with shingles, has been erected in the interior of the grounds. There are various other covered seats, but none of them are good. There is a circular piece of green trelliswork, with gilt balls, which we consider the *ne plus ultra* of bad taste and absurdity. It would disgrace a cockney tea-garden; and the sooner it is swept away from the grounds at Blenheim the better. So much for the details of all that part of what is called the duke's private garden, which lies between the palace and the cascade.

A thousand reflections arise out of the circumstances connected with the present ruinous state of this princely demesne, but we repress them; only observing that the character which we heard of the Duke of Marlborough, in Woodstock and Oxford, is very different indeed from that which the Duke of Wellington bears in the neighbourhood at Strathfieldsaye.

BLENHEIM – 'LOOKING DOWN ON THE LAKE,.....HALF OF IT APPEARED QUITE
GREEN WITH AQUATIC WEEDS.'

OXFORD. —*AUGUST 13.* We passed this day chiefly in looking at the colleges and other public institutions.

The garden of St. John's College is under the care of Mr. Fairbairn, who is introducing various improvements, and intends ultimately to have, if possible, an approximation to an arboretum, with the different species names. This is as it ought to be, and we could wish to see the same thing attempted in every college garden. What all these gardens, without any exception, might excel in, would be, climbers and creepers on their boundary walls, and mignonette in the crevices of their paved open courts, and at the bases of the walls of the gravelled courts.

The walks belonging to Magdalen College are conducted through meadows on raised banks about 30ft. broad, between ditches containing running water, about 10ft. broad and 4ft. deeper than the surface of the meadows. The walk along the centre of the raised bank

121

OXFORD, MAGDALEN COLLEGE – 'THE WALKS BELONGING TO MAGDALEN
COLLEGE ARE CONDUCTED THROUGH MEADOWS ON RAISED BANKS ABOUT 30
FT. BROAD...'

is about 10ft. wide, leaving 10 feet on each side to be varied by trees. Through the framework
formed by the stems of these trees and the undergrowths, the meadows and country beyond
are seen to great advantage; and, in advancing along, so admirably do the trees come in, that
there is not a point, whichever way the eye turns, from which a perfect landscape might not
be transferred to paper. This is saying as much for such a walk as can be said in a landscape
point of view.

122

OXFORD, CHRISTCHURCH, 'THE AVENUE IS MUCH INJURED SINCE WE LAST SAW IT.'

The walks in Christ Church meadow differ from those of Magdalen chiefly in having a greater breadth of turf on each side, and in being more thinly planted with trees; and they might be improved in a similar manner. For the scattered trees in the meadows of both colleges others might be substituted, and added, so as to form an arboretum. Christ Church avenue is much injured since we last saw it, by the decay of the top branches of many of the trees. The area of the quadrangle of Christ Church is a level square of turf, with a basin,

123

(possessing till lately a fountain) in the centre, and surrounded by a broad terrace walk about 3ft. higher than the turf. The sunk area might easily be rendered a most beautiful flower-garden, like that of the Tuileries. In the private garden here are two fig trees, said to have been planted by Cardinal Wolsey, and a very old mulberry tree. The fig trees, which are against a wall, have been cut down so often, that they show no shoots older than twenty of thirty years, and as these proceed from stools concealed by the surface soil, no stranger could discover that the trees are old: in truth, they may rather be considered as suckers from the old trees which formerly stood on the same spot. They bear every year; and, a few days ago, a plate of ripe figs from one of them was exhibited at the Oxford horticultural show. The mulberry tree is a large and venerable fragment, supported by numerous wooden posts, and bound and tied together by iron hoops and rods. The heart wood is entirely rotted out, and the circumferential wood is separated into parts, round each of which the bark is advancing in a manner which promises ultimately to give them the appearance of so many separate natural stems, as we frequently find to be the case in the very old olive plantations in Italy; for example, at Terni.

The kitchen of Christ Church College is 40ft. square and 40ft. high, lighted from a lantern in the centre of the roof. There are three fireplaces, each 20ft. wide; one of which, for roasting, has a grate formed of upright iron bars 4 1/2ft. high, forming a grating about 9in. distant from the brickwork which forms the back of the fireplace. When roasting is to be performed, a vertical stratum of coals is filled in between the grating and the brickwork, and six tiers of spits, each between 13ft. and 14ft. long, and each having on it six or eight joints, or twelve or thirteen fowls, are placed on the racks, and set in motion by the smoke-jack. The dripping from the whole drops into the same dripping-pan, and every separate article is basted with the combined dripping so produced. Thus, if ducks, geese, turkeys, fowls, pork, beef, mutton, venison, veal, and lamb, were all roasting at the same time, each of these articles would be basted with the combined fat of ducks, geese, turkeys, fowls, pork, beef, mutton, venison, veal, and lamb. On expressing our surprise at this to one of the under-cooks who attended us, she informed us that she believed none of the gentlemen knew of the practice; but that the two or three tutors or poorer students who remained during vacations, and who dined sometimes on one joint roasted by itself, expressed their satisfaction at its goodness. It is not a little instructive to reflect on this fact. Here are a number of young men of the first rank and wealth in the kingdom, who affect, and indeed have a right from their station in society, to be epicures, eating what would disgust the humblest mechanic or poorest tradesman. If these frequently dine on meat roasted along with other sorts in a close oven, they are still aware of the difference in flavour between such meat and that roasted by itself in a free current of air; but these noble epicures, who would, no doubt, be shocked beyond measure at the idea of eating meat which had been roasted or baked in a baker's oven, on account of its having been exposed to the exhalations of other kinds of meat supposed to be roasting in it at the same time, are yet faring every day on what is a great deal worse both in reality and idea.

AUGUST 14. We this day looked at the different Oxford nurseries. In 1804, there were only two gardens of this description; that of Mr. Tegg, and that of Mr. Penson. There are now four others. Still the taste at Oxford is more for the sensual, than for the intellectual part of

1. Lilium Tigrinum. 2. Lilium superbum. 3. Lilium Martagon.
4. Lilium Carolinianum. 5. Lilium tenuifolium. 6. Lilium pomponium.
7. Lilium autumnale. 8. Lilium Chalcedonicum.

Day & Haghe, Lith.rs to the Queen.

LILIES, FROM MRS. LOUDON

RHODODENDRON ARBOREUM

gardening. The principal products of all these nurseries are culinary vegetables and fruits; and the next, showy and fragrant flowers. What the gentlemen of the colleges desire most, is what the preacher Huntington says was preferred by the cookmaid at the place where he was gardener, viz. "a flower in a pot, and one that would stand." A geranium, a rose, a night-smelling stock, and mignonette, we were informed, would sell, but not any of the new calceolarias or fuchsias, because in the rooms of the colleges they would not "stand." Forced fruits, such as strawberries and cucumbers, pay remarkably well.

THE BOTANIC GARDEN AT OXFORD is a venerable establishment. It is entered by a noble stone archway, through which is seen a vista to the other extremity of the garden. The two principal hot-houses have elevations of stone, massive and grand in an architectural point of view, but scarcely suitable for preserving plants, much less for growing them. There are two other hot-houses with very steep roofs, adjusted to the angle recommended by Boerhaave as admitting the greatest number of the sun's rays during the winter solstice. The walls of the garden appear to be about 2ft. thick, and 12ft. high, with a coved Gothic cornice on each side, under an elevated Gothic coping. The whole wall is composed of large blocks of smoothly dressed stone, and forms the noblest garden wall, speaking architecturally, which we have seen in any country. Comparing this botanic garden with all the others in Britain, it as far surpasses them in an architectural point of view, as it is inferior to the best of them in

THE BOTANIC GARDEN AT OXFORD – 'IT IS ENTERED BY A NOBLE STONE ARCHWAY, THROUGH WHICH IS SEEN A VISTA TO THE OTHER EXTREMITY OF THE GARDEN.'

129

botanical riches. When we first saw it, in 1804, it was a very poor and apparently neglected garden, hardly worthy of being called botanical; but since it has been put under the direction of Mr. Baxter, the present curator, it has been in all respects wonderfully improved, the number of species, as it appeared to us, has been more than tripled; and the whole is in far better order and keeping.

In the library and museum, Mr. Baxter pointed out to us the herbariums of Gerarde, Dillenius, Morrison, and other old and eminent botanists; the first two volumes of Rudbeck's *Campi Elysii,* folio, full of wood engravings of the plants of all countries, very scarce; this being the only copy of the first volume in England. There are only three copies of

THE BOTANIC GARDEN AT OXFORD – 'COMPARING THIS BOTANIC GARDEN WITH ALL THE OTHERS IN BRITAIN, IT...FAR SURPASSES THEM IN AN ARCHITECTURAL POINT OF VIEW...'

this volume, and six of the second, in the world: all the rest, with the whole of the copies of the remaining ten volumes of the work, were destroyed by fire; and grief for their loss is supposed to have occasioned Rudbeck's death.

Mr. Baxter showed us some leaves of dried specimens prepared for the work on mosses, of which he published three numbers some years ago; but, as Dr. Hooker informs us (*English Flora,* vol. v. p. 130), "the work was never completed, *Mr. Baxter having died* after the third number." We are happy to inform Dr. Hooker and his readers that it was the work only that died, and not the author; for Mr. Baxter now is, as we hope he may long continue to be, in excellent health and spirits. With all Mr. Baxter's knowledge, he is one of the most modest and unassuming of men.

It is much to be regretted that the city of Oxford has not a botanic garden suited to the rank which it holds as a British university. Were a small sum contributed by each of the colleges yearly, even the present garden might be rendered doubly efficient: more especially if the adjoining ground, at present occupied by Mr. Penson, were added to it, and a part or the whole of the meadows of Christ Church. But the situation is altogether bad; and, for a botanic garden worthy of Oxford, a dry, open, ample, airy piece of ground should be selected, outside of the town.

The road to Wantage is through a hilly country, badly cultivated; and it is everywhere in want of having the surface soil deepened by such an instrument as Finlayson's harrow or as Wilkie's grubber; but it will require another and a reading generation of farmers to introduce these implements. We passed only one or two gentlemen's seats, but we observed a number of well-kept cottage gardens, richly ornamented with China roses, hollyhocks, and many of them with georginas. The splendour of the roses on one cottage, in a remote situation, exceeded anything of the kind between it and London: the trees were at least 20ft. high, and were covered with a mass of bloom. We lately saw a lady to whom the present Mr. Lee's grandfather, about forty years ago, showed the first China rose which he had to propagate from, as a great curiosity.

We went down to the Vale of Kennet, in which, on the centre of a broad expanse of the river, where the water is 14ft. deep, is an octagon bathing hut surrounded by a rustic veranda. This is connected with both banks of the river by wooden bridges, from the ends of which proceed gravel walks for fishing from. These lead to a fishing house, and to stews, in which we were shown some remarkably large trout, pike, and numerous eels; and chub, which is only used here for feeding the other fish, though it sometimes sold in London for carp, which it greatly resembles. The scales of this fish were sold, a few years ago, to the London jewellers for 10s. 6d. a pint. We also saw here, for the first time in England, the crawfish, of which we had seen, in 1813, great numbers in the moist meadows on the Vistula at Warsaw and Cracow. They are here in little esteem, and are seldom used, though they are there considered as delicate as shrimps, and are thought to make one of the best soups. We were surprised to find that, though the trout and the pike may be fed advantageously in stews, eels cannot. The manner in which the fish are caught at the weirs here is very simple and ingenious. Below the sluices is placed an iron grating the whole breadth of the stream, and rising nearly to the height of the water in the dam. Beyond the rise it declines into a gutter, which leads to a tank or box at the side. The large fish which are let out by the sluices are thrown over into this gutter, which is also grated, so as to prevent their escaping otherwise than down a slope on one side to the box or chest. In this way as many fish are caught as are wanted, and no more, especially eels.

The Kennet is one of those rivers that exhibit the phenomenon of ice forming in the bottom, and we were informed here by the Earl of Craven's fisherman, that, in severe winters, the ice forms with such rapidity in those parts of the river that are shallow, and where of course, the stream is rapid, that, in one night, a complete dam has been formed across the stream, of such a height as to throw the water over the adjoining banks. The water thus thrown over also freezes, and the consequence would be, a complete inundation of the valley above, if the fishermen did not take effectual means to break up this dam. It is observed that, when the bottom of the river is frozen, one good effect is the result, and this is, that, when it thaws, the pieces of ice, which float up from the bottom, bring all the weeds with them; thus thoroughly cleaning the river.

HIGHCLERE, THE EARL OF CAERNARVON. —AUGUST 14. Whoever has noticed our remarks on the subject of situation, called forth by Bear Wood and by Caversham Park, will readily conceive that we were delighted with the natural features of Highclere. Perhaps, taking the latter altogether, we may venture to call it one of the finest places, as far as ground and wood are concerned, that we have ever beheld.

In proceeding from Newbury to Highclere, the road passes through a richly cultivated country, having in some places a parklike character. In one part, the effect of the trees and turf, on both sides of the road, lead the traveller to believe that he is passing through a park. The road continues in rather a grand style for a cross country road, passing a curious corner clump of larch trees, which, we were informed, constitute the remains of a nursery, and which are now 50ft. high: these trees, small and naked in the stem, look like a gigantic crop of oats, rather than larches; and present a striking example of how much the character of a tree may be changed by the circumstances in which it is grown. Shortly beyond these larches, and apparently forming the termination of a straight line of the road, appears the archway, which is the main entrance into the park of Highclere.

The house is seen, for the first time, when we are about three quarters of a mile distant from it; it is soon lost again, and we do not catch another glimpse of it till we are very near it. Its first appearance is exceedingly grand, standing on an elevated table land, backed by the two hills before mentioned, and commanding a most extensive range of distant country in front. All that we shall farther say of the approach is, that the wood on each side of it is disposed so admirably that there is not a tree that we could wish to alter. The prominences and recesses of the masses correspond with the elevations and declivities of the of the surface in some places, thus following up and increasing the variety indicated by nature; while in others they are found on declivities, so as to create variety and intricacy where none naturally existed. There is scarcely a point, along the whole of this approach, at which an artist might not stop and sketch a landscape that would be well-proportioned in its great component parts; and at least harmonious, if not striking, in its details. The mansion-house, which was much altered within, and entirely cased with Bath stone without, by the late earl, who died in the spring of the year 1833, leaving it unfinished, is a square building, showing three façades, each about 110ft. in extent of frontage. The style of architecture adopted is the Grecian Ionic, as used in the Erectheum at Athens.

In the interior are some good-sized rooms, particularly the library. Notwithstanding all this, we are of opinion, that, to produce a house suitable to the situation, the cheapest and best way would have been to pull the whole down and rebuild it. The views from the house, on the entrance front, are singularly grand. To the right, they command the park scenery, with its high hilly outline of wood as the boundary, and the temple seen rising from a wooded valley. To the left lies the valley of the Kennet, several miles in width; a rich hilly

132

HIGHCLERE, THE GROUNDS

HIGHCLERE, THE GROUNDS

corn country rising beyond. The principal view from the lawn front forms a striking contrast to those already mentioned. In this view we look down to a smooth grassy hollow, and up to the wild woods of Sidon Hill. To the left of this, the Beacon Hill, with its bold outline and bare surface, the latter partially concealed by a wooded eminence rising from the valley right before it, forms a fine contrast to the rich wooded scenery of Sidon. This last mentioned hill is ascended by a spiral drive, partly open, and partly wooded, which terminates unexpectedly in a triumphal arch, through which the eye looks down on the house, the pleasure-ground, and the whole park, as on a map.

Unfavourable circumstances of local climate, which hardly allow an arbutus to protract a wretched existence, induced His Lordship to rely principally upon rhododendrons and azaleas for the decoration of his shrubberies. To extend the garden varieties, and protract the flowering season of the family, became an object which, most actively pursued, has been attended with uncommon success. By means of hybrid intermixture, the season for these beautiful flowers, beginning about the end of April, lasts till the middle of July, almost three months. The very splendid rhododendrons, brilliant to the highest degree with their crimson corollas, of the variety obtained between the Rhododendron arboreum of Nepal and R.

134

HIGHCLERE, THE GROUNDS

catawbiense, and named, by Dr. Lindley, after the Doomsday name of Highclere (Alta-Clera), Rhododendron alta-clerense, come into flower about the third week in April, and are succeeded by a multitude of splendid varieties both of Rhododendron and Azalea, ending with the crosses obtained between Rhododendron maximum and Azalea autumnalis rubra.

Among the herbaceous plants, which were now in splendid beauty, producing most brilliant masses of colour in groups on the lawn, were Lilium tigrinum and L. canadense, and Yucca glaucescens, which has the habit of Y. filamentosa, flowering yearly, but much more freely, with larger and more numerous blossoms, and more elegant foliage. This plant was first given to the nurseries from Highclere. Campanula lactiflora forms a fine lawn plant, either singly or in large masses; the lobelias, georginas, lupines, phloxes, potentillas, asters, gladioluses, petunias, mimuluses, and many of the new Californian plants introduced by Douglas, added to the beauty of the scene. It deserves particularly to be remarked, that the dark purple candy-tuft and Clarkia pulchella form the best masses when mixed with mignonette, and the same may be said of other showy but naked-stemmed annuals; and, farther, that all these flowers, and, in general, all the ornamental shrubs, are introduced in masses; sometimes, as in the case of the snowberry, of one species only; and in

135

others, as in Rubus, Erica, Rhododendron, &c., of several species and varieties of the same genus.

After this slight outline of the leading features of Highclere, it remains for us to give our general opinion of its beauties. Taking it altogether, then, and considering it as a whole, and with reference both to nature and art, we know of no inland place to equal it. There are more striking portions of ground at many places; for example, the brow on which the house is situated at Pain's Hill, with the river below: there are more romantic situations, as at Hafod; situations in which rocks and a natural river have a prominent effect, as at Auchincruive; or rocks without a river, as at Hawkstone: there are more striking situations by art, and where architecture is included; as in the view of Blenheim, on entering the Woodstock gate; or of the enchanted valley, at Alton Towers: but, decidedly, in our opinion, there is no place in England where so much dignity of character, so much elegant variety, and so much cultivated beauty, is preserved throughout a place of such great extent.

LITTLECOT PARK, GENERAL POPHAM. — AUGUST 16. This is a fine old place of the sixteenth century, with both the house and the grounds in perfect preservation. The house lies in a deep secluded bottom of the river Kennet, enclosed by walled gardens; which are surrounded by a park consisting of high ground under turf, and laid out in avenues and lines, chiefly of elms and beeches, in the geometrical style. The approach-road forms an avenue of elms 30 ft. wide and a furlong in length, which brings the stranger to the enriched iron gates in front of the venerable mansion. It is characterised by high roofs covered with tiles, by various gable-ends projecting from them, and by magnificent cathedral-like windows, reaching from the ground to the eaves. Having obtained permission from the general to see

LITTLECOT PARK, 'THIS IS ONE OF THE VERY FEW PLACES WHICH WE HAVE SEEN
WHICH COME ENTIRELY UP TO OUR IDEAS OF HIGH ORDER AND KEEPING.'

the place, we passed onto the kitchen-garden. In this garden, the first things we observed were glass frames, in M.Lindegaard's manner, for ripening peaches and nectarines against the walls, without fire-heat. These frames occasion very little trouble; and the fruit comes in between the forced peaches and those ripened on the garden wall. There are a number of hot-houses and pits, in which pine-apples, melons, and other articles are admirably grown. On one wall there are several apricot trees, which, Mr.Groom, the gardener, informed us, the general considered to be as old as the place: they bear abundantly every year. A branch of the river Kennet passes through the lower part of the garden, in a straight walled canal: thus affording an opportunity of growing excellent watercresses, and of keeping crawfish, eels, and other fish in stews. There is a pond for carp, surrounded by a rockwork or ridge of flints, planted with strawberries, the fruit of which ripens a fortnight or three weeks sooner than that in the open garden.

This is one of the very few places which we have seen which come entirely up to our ideas of high order and keeping, even to the melon-ground and the back sheds. The walks in the flower-gardens are chiefly of turf, and the flower-beds are brimful of soil; so that the line carried round them, though distinct, is perfectly soft and delicate. The grass is smoothly mown; and decayed flowers are pinched off daily by women. The general not only allows as many men and women to be employed as are necessary to keep the place in perfect order, but he pays the men 3s. a week more than is given in the neighbourhood, and allows half-wages during sickness. The gardener here, Mr.Groom, is the son of the gardener to Sir Charles Cockerell, at Seisincote, Gloucestershire: a place which we saw in 1806, when it was highly kept; and which, we are informed, still continues to be one of the best kept places in England. The readers of Sir Walter Scott's works will, no doubt, recollect the singular tradition which he mentions respecting Littlecot Park. The story is related at length in the *Beauties of England and Wales;* and the room in which the tragical scene took place is said to be still in existence. *TOTTENHAM PARK, MARQUESS OF AYLESBURY. —AUGUST 16.* This is an immense place, of which we had heard much; and while, in its immensity and in the general management of the estate, it exceeded our expectations, in its architecture and gardening, which we had heard most praised, it fell short of them. The estate consists of 60,000 acres in a ring fence, one and a half of which, we suppose, may consist of the ancient forest of Savernake, said to be the largest in Britain in the possession of a private individual, with the house in the centre.

The park may be described as an interminable oak forest, on a surface which, taken as whole, may be considered flat, but which, in particular places, exhibits undulations. This forest is crossed at right angles by two avenues, one above eleven miles long, which intersect each other in the centre, at which point of intersection is placed the house. A stranger can form no idea either of the extent of the park or of the length of the avenues; so that to him the characteristic of the place is interminableness. Besides these principal avenues, there are innumerable subordinate ones, many planted with beech trees, and others cut out of the forest and bordered by the native oaks and birches. There is one master avenue, or rather grass drive, which makes a circuit of the entire forest, and which is 25 miles long.

In the bottom of one quiet valley in Savernake Lodge, a small villa, intended for the oldest son of the family when he marries, with grounds about it very neatly laid out, and well kept. Here the children of the present marquess were nursed up by Mrs.Morgan, the present

TOTTENHAM PARK – 'THIS IS AN IMMENSE PLACE OF WHICH WE HAD HEARD MUCH.'

housekeeper, and each child had its garden. These gardens still exist, and appear like little islands in a sea of turf. They are surrounded by hedges, and are still kept up with great care and taste, under the direction of Mrs. Morgan.

The mansion strikes a stranger as being placed in a low situation, as the grounds rise slightly from it on every side. It was originally, we believe, designed or built by Lord Burlington, in the Palladian style of course, with a centre, and two wings joined by segmental corridors; a most unsuitable style, according to modern ideas, for a baronial residence in the centre of an ancient forest. This house has for some years past been undergoing renovations, and receiving additions in the same general style; but we regret to say that we never in the whole course of our observation met with any thing more unsatisfactory, either exteriorly or within. The chief fault lies in the works having been begun apparently without any general plan. In whichever way the exterior elevation is viewed, it is without grandeur.

The small size of the windows, also, makes the rooms appear gloomy and dark, and this, contrasted with their gorgeous French furniture, gave us more the idea of princely tombs (such as we have seen in vaults of Petersburg and Konigsberg, covered with rich furs and velvet, and with a profusion of gilding), than of cheerful sleeping-rooms. There is nothing that takes away from the idea of habitableness and enjoyment so much as overlaying things with ornament. Coming out of these rooms, one is really quite astonished at the meagre finishing of the hall and principal staircase. There is a wing containing a Doric conservatory, the columns hollow, and their flutings filled in with glass; the triglyphs and other parts of the frieze are also filled in with glass: conceits most unhappily at variance with

Doric simplicity and elegance. Adjoining this, but not joined to it, and evidently an after-thought, is an architectural orangery with an opaque roof, higher than the other, and sufficiently discordant with it to harmonise with the rest of the place. It is not yet finished, and, were it not for the sake of Mr. Burns's fine orange trees, we should be tempted to wish it never may. There is a terrace, connecting these appendages with the main body of the house, from which a flight of steps descends to the flower-garden.

The house-porter here, Joseph Shindle, is a remarkable instance of the force of native genius. In spite of his morning duties of wheeling in coals and wood, and wheeling out ashes and dirt, he has contrived to make a number of curious sundials and barometers; and to paint several pictures of fruits and flowers, and make frames for them. He is an excellent cabinet-maker and joiner, and a theoretical as well as practical astronomer. He has contrived, out of his savings, to collect a tolerable library, including Hutton's *Mathematical Dictionary* in quarto.

There is one fine circumstance connected with Tottenham Park, which deserves to be mentioned for the credit of its liberal and benevolent lord. It is open at all times to the inhabitants of the surrounding towns; who drive, ride, or make gipsy-parties in it at pleasure. *The Grange, Alexander Baring, Esq. —August 19.* The road to this place, over a country of downs, is dreary, and very uninteresting to a stranger. Andover, like an oasis in a desert, is a neat and clean town, affording a good and cheap inn (the White Hart); but there are several miserable heartless- looking villages between that place and the long approach which leads to the Grange. The house here, however, repays all the trouble; and we have not seen a mansion the external elevation of which pleased us so much, since we commenced our tour. The beauties of this place lie in a narrow winding valley, with a small stream in the bottom, which spreads into a broad expanse of water near the house. The latter is proudly situated on a steep bank, supported by a grand architectural terrace, and that again by a massive terrace of gravel and turf, with a third smaller terrace, of the same materials, below. The main body of the house is in the Doric style with a portico at one end, and a loggia with square columns on each side, by Wilkins; with a secondary mass, and a conservatory in the Ionic style, by R. C. Cockerell.

Its temple-like magnificence must be seen to be felt; and, indeed, it will repay any one who has a taste for architecture, to travel a hundred miles out of his way to see it. We shall never forget the first impression made on us by the Doric portico, when we saw it from the road to the kitchen-garden, on the bank forming the opposite side of the valley. The Ionic conservatory is the finest thing of the kind in England; and, in our opinion, far surpasses those of Syon and of Alton Towers. Its characteristics are simplicity and grandeur.

THE GRANGE – 'ITS TEMPLE-LIKE MAGNIFICENCE MUST BE SEEN TO BE FELT;
AND, INDEED, IT WILL REPAY ANY ONE WHO HAS A TASTE FOR ARCHITECTURE,
TO TRAVEL A HUNDRED MILES OUT HIS WAY TO SEE IT.'

THE GRANGE – 'WE SHALL NEVER FORGET THE FIRST IMPRESSION MADE ON US
BY THE DORIC PORTICO WHEN WE SAW IT FROM THE ROAD...'

We cannot help admiring the Grange as one of the noblest of British villas. The approach to the entrance front is through an avenue of lime trees, 100ft. wide, and twice as many years old; having, as we are informed, been planted in the time of Inigo Jones, who built the first house, nearly on the present site, for Lord Chancellor Hyde.

On the road from Ringwood to Wimborne Minster are some extensive plantations of pinasters, which, on the poorest soils, grow faster than either the Scotch pine or the larch. To the right of the public road is Canford House, on the banks of the Avon, a monastic Gothic building, among fine old trees. It has a charming effect from the road. The minster at Wimborne would afford a fine study for the antiquary, as would many of the chimney tops of the houses in the town to the modern architect. In some of the streets, vines, climbing roses, honeysuckles, and even herbaceous flowers, are planted in the crevices of the pavement, and trained up against the houses. These flowers, some small flower-gardens hardly fenced, and the lead hanging from the eaves of the church, speak favourably of the manners and morals of the people.

AUGUST 27. —FROM WIMBORNE, THROUGH BLANDFORD, TO SHAFTESBURY. The greater part of the road to Blandford is over naked downs, steep chalky hills succeeding to valleys all the way. The country on both sides is most fatiguing to the eye of every one but a fox-hunter. Iris fœtidissima is abundant by the road side. The road from Blandford to Shaftesbury is through a fine country, but it is extremely hilly.

BRYANSTON HOUSE, J. PORTMAN, ESQ. — The house, like that of Langton, is in a bottom, with the meadows of the Stour and a fine reach of the river in front; but is placed much higher, backed by steeper hills, and commands much bolder ground on the opposite side of the river.

BRYANSTON HOUSE – 'THIS PLACE IS AT ALL TIMES OPEN TO ALL THE DECENTLY
DRESSED INHABITANTS OF BLANDFORD.'

This place is at all times open to all the decently dressed inhabitants of Blandford, and to all other respectable persons. The grassy terraces, called the cliff walks, are scenes of extraordinary dignity and beauty. Besides the views of the river, the park, the country beyond the bridge, and the town of Blandford, they display in the foreground some fine specimens of exotic trees, and of yews, boxes and hollies; the surface of the ground was in some places covered with vigorous plants of scolopendrium, and in others with beds of native violets and primroses. In spring the whole of the native woods of this place must afford a rich treat to the botanist, and lover of native flowers.

STOURHEAD, SIR RICHARD COLT HOARE, BART.—This celebrated place is so well known, that we shall make no attempt to describe it. Alfred's Tower is distinctly seen from Shaftesbury, and, indeed, from the rising grounds for twenty miles round on every side. Such towers are always sources of gratification in a country; they afford pleasure to every traveller, and in that respect, they are altogether more noble objects than those temples and other garden buildings, which afford pleasure to, or, perhaps more correctly speaking, are seen only by, the occupier or visitants of the place. Stourhead may be characterised as a fine specimen of country residences of the old school of modern gardening, as well in the manner of laying it out, as in the style of keeping it up. There is a good deal of formality and quaintness mixed with fine natural features in this place; formality in the regular cutting of the undergrowths and hedges of laurels, which, as a lady who accompanied us observed, looked like beds of gigantic moss, and overgrown hedges of box; and quaintness in the continuance of the overconspicuous and superfluously high stone bridge, and the numerous temples and statues. The obelisk, also, with the gilt sun over it, and the monastery with its spire like

STOURHEAD.

chimney top, might be adduced in support of this opinion. However, the basis of the whole remains the same as it was originally; and with a certain degree of remodeling in the walks and in the undergrowths, for the place is rendered monotonous by the prevalence of laurel, and the addition of modern choice trees and shrubs, Stourhead might still hold its rank as one of the first in the island.

Of late years, a number of rhododendrons have been distributed over the grounds; but they are dotted in too equidistant a manner, and in a few years if they are not removed, will destroy all breadth of effect in the lawn. It would have been better to have substituted them for part of the common laurels, which, as we have before observed, are much too abundant for scenery of so limited an extent, and which give a sameness to the woods unworthy of a place presenting in other respects so much beauty. Two thirds at least of these laurels ought to be removed, and their place supplied by rhododendrons and other American shrubs; and by box, holly and yew. This would be nothing more than acting in the spirit of the original planter, laurels being, about the middle of the last century, as choice as rhododendrons are now.

These points attended to, and the ornamental buildings put into thorough repair, the valley of lakes at Stourhead would form a scene of great and unique beauty. Nothing can be finer than the first impression made by the water a few paces within the entrance from the inn. The guide-book informs us that we ought to enter from the lawn front of the house; but this we found impracticable. The church and churchyard are pleasingly situated on a sloping bank, and the churchyard is one of the best kept which are to be seen in England. Roses and other flowering shrubs are planted against the church; cypresses and other trees are sprinkled among the graves, and the grass is kept as smooth as any lawn. The tombs of the Hoare family are in an open chapel at one end of the church, and the tombs of their stewards at the other, the latter containing the remains of three generations of the same family. The fence is a sunk wall with its perpendicular side towards the church, so that at a short distance there appears to be no fence at all, and the whole seems a component part of the pleasure-ground. We have seldom seen anything so well managed. There is a handsome circular stone seat [near this], which the guide informed us the present baronet built to enable the country people, while waiting till the service began, to sit down in the open air, rather than to go into

STOURHEAD – 'THERE IS A GOOD DEAL OF FORMALITY AND QUAINTNESS.'

the damp church. To prevent this dampness, a hint might be taken from the practice of Ringwood.

The drive at Stourhead, which is said to be six miles in extent, displays some fine woods and extensive prospects; but the ascents are too steep to be enjoyed by those who, like us, travel with only one horse. The table-land on which the tower stands having been gained, nearly level, and covered with soft turf, is one of the finest things of the kind in the kingdom. The view extends over many miles, and into several counties. One of the finest features about any extensive place which is hilly, or contains a high hill, such as Stourhead or High Clere, is a smooth road which shall ascend almost insensibly, and by a beautiful route to the top of the hill, and descend again equally agreeably by a different road. There is no hill that exists in which this effect may not be accomplished; and of this ascent and descent of the Simplon is a standing proof.

It is but justice to state that every part of Stourhead was uniformly well kept; not in what is entitled to be called high keeping, because the edges of the walks and roads were harsh and disagreeable, and some things were going to decay; but, with these exceptions, we have no fault to find.

AUGUST 28.—HINDON The occasional glimpses caught of Fonthill from the high parts of the open downs, surrounded by woods, and without a single human habitation, a fence, or a made road appearing in the landscape, convey to a stranger a correct impression of the character of the place; viz., that of a monastic building in a wild, hilly, and thinly inhabited

OLD WARDOUR CASTLE AND FONTHILL

IN HERTFORDSHIRE

FONTHILL – 'OCCASIONAL GLIMPSES CAUGHT...CONVEY TO A STRANGER A
CORRECT IMPRESSION OF THE CHARACTER; VIZ., THAT OF A MONASTIC
BUILDING IN A WILD, HILLY, AND THINLY INHABITED COUNTRY...'

country, such as we may imagine to have existed three or four centuries ago. On arriving at the miserable town of Hindon, its appearance serves rather to heighten than to lessen this impression; without trade or manufacture, and with no main road passing through it, it contains only a few houses the largest of which assume the character of inns; but of these inns the best does not even take in a newspaper. Till the passing of the Reform Bill, Hindon derived its support chiefly from the return of the members to parliament; but this resource being gone, the inhabitants are now in the greatest misery. Before Mr. Beckford sold Fonthill, he generously gave 20 acres to the poorest inhabitants for ever as garden ground; observing as it is said, that they had need of a friend.

FONTHILL ABBEY; H. BENNETT, ESQ.—This place, independantly of the historical associations connected with the name of Beckford, well deserves to be visited by every person who takes an interest respecting, or is desirous of improving himself in, landscape-gardening; because it is the only one in England, in which he will find the most perfect unity of character preserved

149

FONTHILL – 'AFTER THE ABBEY WAS COMMENCED HE WAS SO IMPATIENT TO GET
IT FINISHED, THAT HE KEPT REGULAR RELAYS OF MEN AT WORK NIGHT AND
DAY, INCLUDING SUNDAYS.'

throughout the grounds, and that character one belonging to an age long since past in this country, and only now to be found in certain mountainous regions of Catholic countries on the continent. The chief object of Mr. Beckford seems to have been to impress this character on all the great leading features of Fonthill, and only to have modern artificial scenes, as occasional episodes. Hence there is not a single gravel walk or made road about the place; nor in the immediate vicinity of the house is there an exotic tree, shrub or flower, save an apricot and a fig tree, planted against the south side of the grand entrance, as we may suppose by some monk who had brought the seeds of these fruits from some Italian or Swiss monastery.

The appearance of the abbey character being complete, in the general expression, the next point to be studied is the extent and the manner in which Mr. Beckford introduced modern improvements in the grounds: this was exceedingly simple. He confined himself entirely to the introduction of exotic trees and shrubs in secluded places only; and these he disposed in what may be called by-scenes in the woods, in such a manner as that a person who knew nothing of trees could never suspect that they were not natives.

There was an American ground in the place, consisting of many of the trees and shrubs of that country, disposed in groups and thickets, as if they had sprung up naturally, with glades of turf kept smoothly mown to admit of walking through among them, and examining their separate beauties. There was a rose-ground, a thornery, and a pinetum treated in the same manner; but, along the numerous walks and drives, the common trees and shrubs of the country were those principally introduced. The next point of study is the

FONTHILL – 'MR BECKFORD PURSUED THE OBJECTS OF HIS WISHES, WHATEVER
THEY WERE, NOT COOLLY AND CONSIDERATELY LIKE MOST OTHER MEN, BUT
WITH ALL THE ENTHUSIASM OF PASSION.'

manner of conducting the walks and drives. There was, first, from the end of the grand avenue, a broad carriage drive of several miles in length, which made a circuit of the whole place, and displayed the finest views of the abbey and the surrounding country. The greater part of this country is sufficiently naked to keep up the idea of a past age; and the tower at Stourhead, and the woods of Wardour Castle, are sufficiently distinct not to counteract this impression. Within this outer drive there is a park wall that encloses nearly 600 acres, the greater part of which is covered with wood, but with innumerable grassy glades, and some small lakes. Through this scenery, subordinate drives have been formed to the extent, as it is said in the *Guide-Book*, of 27 miles. Two small garden episodes may be mentioned: one a herb garden, containing such plants as we may suppose the monks might have cultivated to use in medicine; and the other a garden (which, when we saw it in 1807, had a small hot-house in it, not much bigger than a cucumber frame) for a favourite dwarf. The kitchen-garden was in the outer park, about a mile and a half from the abbey, and was only seen from one part of the grand drive.

We have spoken thus far of Fonthill as it was, or as it may be supposed to have been, during its occupation by Mr. Beckford; and we have done so partly from our recollections of what it was when we first saw it, in 1807, through the kindness of Mr. Milne, the gardener at that time, and partly from its present state; but the reader will recollect, that the greater part of the abbey is now in ruins, and all the interesting parts of the grounds (unless we except the grand avenue and drive, and the American grounds) are in such a state of neglect, as hardly to be recognised for what they were in 1807. To preserve the abbey from falling was impossible, from the nature of its construction; but it is deeply to be regretted that the grounds have fallen into hands which, from some cause or other, could suffer the ruin to extend to them.

We spent the greater part of two days in looking over this place, even to the cottages and cottage-gardens in the village; and, having met with some of the old men who had worked on the grounds during the whole of Mr. Beckford's time, we indulged ourselves in asking questions, and procured much curious information respecting the building of the abbey, the mode of life of Mr. Beckford while he resided in it, the falling down of the tower in Mr. Farquhar's time, and the general effect of Mr. Beckford's immense expenditure on the surrounding population.

It appears that Mr. Beckford pursued the objects of his wishes, whatever they were, not coolly and considerately like most other men, but with all the enthusiasm of passion. No sooner did he decide upon any point, than he had it carried into immediate execution, whatever might be the cost. After the abbey was commenced, he was so impatient to get it finished, that he kept regular relays of men at work night and day, including Sundays; supplying them liberally with ale and spirits while they were at work, and when any thing was completed, which gave him particular pleasure, adding an extra 5l. or 10l. to be spent on drink. The first tower, the height of which from the ground was 400ft., was built of wood, in order to see its effect: this was then taken down, and the same form put up in wood covered in cement. This fell down, and the tower was built a third time, on the same foundation, with brick and stone. The foundation of the tower was originally that of a small summer-house, to which Mr. Beckford was making additions when the idea of the abbey occurred to him; and this idea he was so impatient to realise, that he could not wait to remove the summer- house, to make a proper foundation for the tower, but carried it up on the walls already standing.

In confirmation of our idea that Mr. Beckford's enjoyments consisted of a succession of violent impulses, we may mention that, when he wished a new walk to be cut in the woods, or any work of that kind to be done, he used to say nothing about it in the way of preparation, but merely gave orders, perhaps late in the afternoon, that it should be cleared out and in a perfect state by the following morning at the time he came out to take his ride. The whole strength of the village was then put in requisition, and employed during the night; and the next day, when Mr. Beckford came to inspect what was done, if he was pleased with it, he used to give a 5l. or a 10l. note to the men who had been employed to drink, besides, of course, paying their wages, which were always liberal.

These are but a few of the numerous tales which were told us by different persons about Fonthill; and it must be recollected that we do not vouch for the truth of any of them, though we think the whole of them are very likely to be true. We admire in Mr. Beckford his vivid imagination and cultivated mind, and that good taste in landscape-gardening which produced the perfect unity of character which pervades the grounds at Fonthill. We also give him full credit for his good sense in having quitted the place when he could no longer afford to keep it up, and the honourable principle he showed in never getting into debt, but paying liberal prices and ready money to the last. We must, however, enter our protest against the recklessness with which he employed his wealth to gratify his wishes, without regard to its demoralising effects on the labouring population of his neighbourhood, effects so serious that it will take a generation to remove them.

AUGUST 30. — WARDOUR CASTLE; THE EARL OF ARUNDEL. — This place takes its name from the very fine ruins of the original castle; but the modern mansion is a plain Grecian edifice with wings, without a portico to its main entrance, and not only objectionable as a piece of architecture, but as unconnected with the grounds either by mural appendages, or sufficient woody scenery. It contains a Grecian chapel, which is much admired; but, for our own taste, we have never seen a chapel either in Italy or England in that taste which can be compared with those in the Gothic manner. Looking from the garden front, there is a very nobly wooded ridge, nearly a mile in length, which forms the boundary to the landscape on the left, and to the right other woods, corresponding in extent, though on less elevated ground. At

WARDOUR CASTLE – 'THIS PLACE TAKES ITS NAME FROM THE VERY FINE RUINS
OF THE ORIGINAL CASTLE; BUT THE MODERN MANSION IS A PLAIN GRECIAN
EDIFICE WITH WINGS.'

the bottom of the wooded ridge is seen the ruins of the ancient castle, and, in front, a lawn of great extent leads the eye to an artificial river. The fine feature of the place is the terrace walk or drive, a mile in length, on the side of the wooded ridge. It has been originally planted with oaks, silver firs, elms, beeches, hollies, and some other trees, with a general under-growth of laurel; so that in the winter season it must be particularly cheerful. The views from it, down the steep grassy slopes between the trees to the ruins, the modern house, the extensive lawns, and the water, (here seen to the greatest advantage), or over the trees to the distant country, with the hills in the horizon, are grand, varied, and interesting. In these views, Fonthill, and the tower at Stourhead, are striking objects.

SEPTEMBER 2. —*STONEHENGE.* — This ruin of what may be considered a primeval temple of philosophy, of religion, of devotion, or of instruction (for all these we consider to be essentially the same), affords some good hints for garden buildings on a large scale. A circle of pillars, whether square or round, on a large scale, joined by massive architraves, either with or without cornices, is a noble and imposing object, and would be so even if the pillars were built of brick, and covered with Roman cement. Such an ornament might form a fine termination to a wooded hill; and we do not believe there are any which would produce so grand an effect for so small a sum. The ruins of Stonehenge, though exceedingly interesting in an antiquarian point of view, are very deficient in architectural interest. We met here with an artist, Mr. Browne of Amesbury, author of *An Illustration of Stonehenge and Abury*. He was sitting in a kind of covered wheelbarrow, the bottom of which formed his seat; a box, which

154

served as the feet of the wheelbarrow, protected his legs, and kept his feet from the ground, while from the sides and back were continued up glazed canvas, so as to form a complete box. In the sides are two very small circular panes of glass, serving as spy holes. The machine is worthy the attention of other rural artists.

WILTON HOUSE; EARL OF PEMBROKE. —Through a lobby we proceed to an entrance hall open to the roof, like that at Fonthill, at the end of which there is a flight of five or six steps, which lead to a cloister, which surrounds a square open court. This cloister contains an extensive collection of antique sculptures, including statues, busts, therms, and relievos. We believe there is scarcely a more extensive collection in England than that in this cloister, and in the other parts of the house, though there are more costly articles in the sculpture galleries at Woburn Abbey and Deepdene. There are a number of good rooms, and in particular the saloon, which is a double cube of 30ft. on the side. The ceiling of this room is coved, and the measurement of 30ft. is not from the floor to the cornice, but to the highest part. The views from the windows to the grounds give no adequate idea of the extent of the park, because the latter is too much crowded with trees near the house, and because there is an architectural seat, very improperly placed as a termination to a short broad walk, conveying the idea to a stranger that there is a public road, or some interruption, or object to be concealed behind.

The view to the Palladian bridge, and that to the fine old cedars is good, and is heightened in effect by the rising grounds in the distance, well clothed with wood. The view from the library to the architectural flower-garden is the best of its kind; in the centre walk

STONEHENGE – 'WE MET HERE WITH AN ARTIST, MR BROWNE OF AMESBURY...HE WAS SITTING IN A KIND OF COVERED WHEELBARROW, THE BOTTOM OF WHICH FORMED HIS SEAT.'

there is a fountain, and it terminates at the distance of several hundred yards in a building from a design by Hans Holbein, which was once the entrance porch to the house. It is in the impure Grecian style of that artist's time. In descending from the house to the grounds, the first cause of regret is the want of an architectural basement, but ill atoned for by placing some pedestals and vases on the naked grass. The flower-garden alluded to has an excellent general effect; the descent to it is by a broad flight of steps from the library, and it has one one side an open pillared building, elevated so as to command a view of the whole garden, and of the park scenery beyond. This scenery consists chiefly of cedars in the foreground; and their effect, in connexion with the fountain, and with the cases and other objects in the flower-garden, has a grand and Oriental air. The walks in the garden are bordered with yew tree boards rounded on the edges, instead of stone: these have been found to last ten years without repair. The beds are overgrown with shrubs or otherwise in an unsuitable state, the family not having resided here for several years.

Formerly the inhabitants of Wilton had the right of walking along the banks of the river in the park, but they are not entirely excluded, and can only by a very especial favour procure a sight of the house or grounds. The inhabitants are quite aware of the injustice which has been done them in excluding them from their ancient rights of walking by the side of the river in the park; but so powerful is a wealthy family in a small country place, that neither the corporation of Wilton united, nor any individual among them, would incur the risk of reclaiming public right.

WILTON HOUSE – '...A BUILDING FROM A DESIGN BY HANS HOLBEIN, WHICH WAS
ONCE THE ENTRANCE PORCH TO THE HOUSE. IT IS IN THE IMPURE GRECIAN
STYLE OF THAT ARTIST'S TIME.'

4

CASHIOBURY PARK,

ASHRIDGE PARK, WOBURN ABBEY

AND

HATFIELD HOUSE

OCTOBER 1825

RECALLED IN 1835

Our esteemed friend Mr. Britton, who is about to publish *A Topographical and Descriptive Account of Cashiobury*, having asked us if we could supply any information respecting the gardens, we are induced to print the present article, which was prepared exactly as it is in Nov., 1825; with the exception of the additions contained within brackets. These additions are made entirely from the Return Paper filled up for us by the gardener at Cashiobury, Mr. Anderson. The whole is very far from being a correct idea of the gardens at Cashiobury; but, not having time to revisit it at present, we consider it our duty to supply what we have to Mr. Britton, leaving him to choose any part of it, or reject the whole, as he may think proper.

OCTOBER 13, 1825. LONDON TO WATFORD AND BERKHAMSTEAD. — Proceeding along the Edgware Road, we found it had undergone great improvement within the last three or four years. This road needed no alteration in the direction, being nearly a straight line from Paddington to Edgware; but it was very irregular in regard to breadth; and some hills required lowering, and hollow places and trifling watercourses filling up, or being crossed by substantial bridges. All these improvements, and others, have been accomplished in a very effectual and satisfactory manner, under the direction of the local trustees. At Edgware, there is one of the handsomest toll-houses in the neighbourhood of London. On the summit of the tower is a reflecting lamp with three burners; two looking along the road before and behind, and one looking across for the purpose of illuminating the gate and gate-posts. (The tower on this toll-house has been since taken down, the lamp at night having been found to frighten horses, when brilliantly illuminated. Such, at least, was the excuse made to us, in 1834, for its disappearance.)

CASHIOBURY PARK, THE SEAT OF THE EARL OF ESSEX, has been celebrated for upwards of a century and a half, for its plantations and gardens. We entered the park through a recently erected Gothic gateway and lodge, built, as we were informed, from the proprietor's own designs. The style was that sort of Elizabethan Gothic which prevails in the house.

Cashiobury House, and the scenery immediately surrounding it, excite ideas of

CASHIOBURY PARK — 'GRANDEUR, COMBINED WITH COMFORT AND BEAUTY.'

158

CASHIOBURY PARK — 'HAS BEEN CELEBRATED FOR UPWARDS OF A CENTURY
AND A HALF.'

grandeur, combined with comfort and beauty, such as cannot easily be communicated by words. The buildings and garden scenery seem peculiarly well suited to each other, both are venerable with age, extensive, rich in design, and generally in the highest order and keeping. We entered the pleasure-ground by a small door near a Turkish pavilion, richly lined with cloth, and carpeted and furnished with sofa and tables. We then passed in front of the house, and entered on the other side to a series of different sorts of flower-gardens. After passing through these in succession, the effect left on the mind was that of having been carried through a labyrinth of beauty and variety. So rapidly were we hurried along, that, after a first visit, it is not easy to recall to the memory distinct pictures of what we have seen, or the order in which we saw them. We shall merely note a few particulars from recollection, promising ourselves, in the beginning of next summer, the gratification of seeing this place at leisure, when to its many other attractions will be added the singing of innumerable birds.

Much of the gardening and botanical interest of all pleasure-grounds consists in the

159

exotic trees and shrubs which they contain. There are some fine specimens of this kind in these gardens: one of the oldest plants of the Magnolia tripetala in England (in 1835, 14ft. high); a very large Magnolia grandiflora (one against a wall, 50ft. high); and some of M. conspicua in the open air: but the largest plant was in the Chinese conservatory; where, however, it has not a tenth part of the room requisite to its attaining its full size. There are some magnificent and venerable plants of Rhododendron, Azalea, and Andromeda. The American plants, in general, are grouped together in dug masses, surrounded by turf; and they have grown to such a size as totally to cover the margin of the dug space around them, and to form a broken picturesque outline on the turf. Roses and ornamental flowers are also disposed in masses, much in the same way as at Cobham Hall, in Kent. Some are enclosed by basket-work, others trail over rocks and fantastic stones; some of the rockeries have a margin of curious Derbyshire spar, and others are entirely of plum-pudding stone. There are groups of large shells (Chama gigas), corals, corallines, madrepores, tuffa, lava, petrifactions,

CASHIOBURY PARK — 'TWO LARGE GRANITE BALLS ATTRACT THE EYE.'

ammonites, and different sorts of scoria, all curiously intermixed with flowers and plants. There is a picturesque aquarium, the sides of which are finely ornamented with rockwork and American evergreens. There is a conservatory with an opaque roof in the ancient style, with the piers between the windows externally clothed with rare exotic creepers, and the interior of the house decorated with rustic props, and green trellis-work. At one end is a sort of banqueting room, carpeted and furnished with couches, sofas, tables, musical instruments, books (especially on botany and landscape), mirrors, and a variety of other things.

The plants in the conservatory are chiefly orange trees, which are particularly appropiate to this kind of building: they are not, generally, in tubs, but planted in the free soil; and they look better than could have been expected from plants kept perpetually under an opaque roof. The Chinese garden here is unique of its kind. It is not large, but contains a conservatory, a sort of low pagoda, and other ornamental buildings, and a great quantity of

CASHIOBURY PARK, IN THE GROUNDS

CASHIOBURY PARK, IN THE GROUNDS

valuable Chinese porcelain, of Chinese figures, monsters, mandarins, the god Joss, dragons, &c., and paintings, fountains, gold fish, jets, &c. In the conservatory are all the sorts of camellias that could be procured when it was planted; very large plants of green and black tea, because at that time it was not known that green tea is nearly as hardy as the sweet bay (Laurus nobilis), and will, in a few years, be a common evergreen in our shrubberies in the south of England.

We could say a great deal more about these grounds; but the truth is, we were so much charmed with them, that we have not a sufficiently definite recollection of what we saw; and doubt not that inaccuracies, and, of course, omissions, will be found in what we have said. A fine effect on the mind is produced where, in passing from one garden to another, two large granite balls attract the eye. A copperplate inscription informs us that they were shot from the castle of Abydos, in the Dardanelles, and fell on a ship under the command of a brother of Lord Essex, in the squadron of Admiral Duckworth, and killed or wounded 15 men. They weigh 7 cwt. each. The unexpected occurrence of objects of this sort recall the mind from what it is engaged in, and relieve it by raising up a new train of ideas, and transporting the imagination to distant and very different scenes. Such episodical effects are very desirable, when they can be introduced in garden scenery without appearing ridiculous or affected.

The kitchen-garden at Cashiobury is large; but not more so than is required for the family, which resides here all the year, and averages at least a hundred persons. As an item of

CASHIOBURY PARK, TREES IN THE GROUNDS

consumption, the gardener, Mr. Anderson, informed us, that he had sent in last year ten thousand heads of celery. On one of the walls we observed two plum trees, which had been killed down to the graft by a *coup de soleil,* one afternoon about 2 o'clock, in July, 1825. The trees were in their usual state when Anderson passed them, about half-past 1 o'clock; and when he returned, in half an hour, he found all their foliage black.

At Cashiobury, we found long ranges of frames filled with endive, brown Cos lettuce, and large quantities, also, of full-grown endive, placed in the floors of the vineries and peach-houses, not in a state of forcing, but of slow or imperceptible growth, amounting almost to complete hybernation. There was also a large plot of chicory for the purpose of

being dug up during winter, and forced into leaf in any warm dark shed or cellar, in the Dutch, Belgic, German, and Russian manner. Two of three hot-beds were already filled with pots of Neapolitan violets, which are here regularly forced throughout the whole winter, their blossoms being much in demand for perfuming apartments.

Without viewing the park, we took our leave by an approach not far from the kitchen-garden; to which, as a lodge, there is a very picturesque cottage, in the old style of oak framing, filled up with brickwork, and plastered. This lodge, like the other, is also from the design of the proprietor, and does credit to his taste.

The head-gardener here had lately been visiting Stowe, and other remarkable gardens within a day or two's ride of Cashiobury. He mentioned that, in the months of September and October, a gardener could better spare time for this purpose than at any other season of the year. This practice of gardeners visiting one another's gardens ought to be particularly encouraged by their employers; for scarcely any other means will be found so effectual in improving them, and enabling them to add to the stock of plants, and increase the variety and excellence of what is under their care.

OCTOBER 14. BERKHAMPSTEAD TO WOBURN. — We went from Berkhampstead to Ashridge Park along an excellent new road which leads across the country to Dunstable, and was formed, as were told, chiefly, or entirely, at the expense of the late Earl of Bridgewater. Various other roads leading to Ashridge were made by the same patriotic individual, who, in this respect, may be said to have displayed a similarity of taste with his ancestor, the celebrated Duke of Bridgewater, the friend and patron of Brindley, the engineer. We entered the park by a very elegant Gothic lodge, built of rubbed white stone and black flints. No one is allowed to enter or go out by this or any other of the gates, without having his name and address put down in a book kept by the porter. An excellent approach road, the length of

ASHRIDGE PARK.

MAGNOLIA TRIPETALA

WOBURN ABBEY – THE TERRACE GARDEN

A HERTFORDSHIRE LANE

168

which is reckoned by miles, leads over an even surface, and through a stately grove, composed chiefly of beech trees, to the house. Every variety of effect is produced that can result from a varied disposition of the trees; and groups, thickets, scattered trees and bushes, ferns, furze, hollies, thorns, glades, recesses, and natural vistas, succeed each other in endless variety. These were interspersed with abundance of red and fallow deer in some places, and horses and cattle in others. No distant prospect, nor any striking object, meets the eye till we are within half a furlong of the house. This grand and irregular pile is seen to very good advantage from this and the Dunstable approach. The two prominent features in the outline are, a square tower near one end, and a lofty spire with a clock at the other. From the two approaches mentioned, these two features fall into perspective in such a way as to form one pile, or group; but when the edifice, or, rather, assemblage of edifices, is viewed directly either from the entrance or garden front, it appears thrown into two groups. Though it does not, when so viewed, form so good a whole, yet it gives an idea of grandeur and magnificence to an ordinary observer, which, perhaps, would not be produced by the foreshortening of an angular perspective view.

We first went to see the kitchen-garden, which is upwards of a mile from the house. On our way to it, we descended to a hollow surface, and passed through scenery of a more open and varied description than that of the Berkhampstead approach. The timber trees were, if possible, grander than before: both oaks and beeches had straight clean trunks, often, we have little doubt, 50ft. or 60ft. high.

We found the head kitchen-gardener, Mr. Torbron, advantageously known at Kew, and by a paper on forcing cherries in the *London Horticultural Society's Transactions*, busily occupied in making up that day's supply for the kitchen and the dessert. A large sheet of paper has a printed column down the left-hand margin, enumerating every description of kitchen-garden product, each article having a line ruled across the page; then there is a vertical column for every day in the month, headed as in the table below, with the days of the week. Fifty-two of these printed sheets are required for the year. The first thing the gardener does, is to enter in the table, under the day of the month, and day of the week, the articles he is about to send off; noting such things as are sent by weight or measure, by inserting their weight or measure after them; but simply inserting the number in figures when the articles are sent by number: thus:

January Sent on ∴	1st Friday	2d Saturday	3d Sunday	4th Monday
Potatoes –	2 pecks common 1 pk. kidneys	3 pecks common	3 pecks common	2 pecks common 1 peck kidneys
Melons –	2 Cantaloups	1 green flesh 1 black rock		2 Lady Chite's green flesh
Grapes –	2 lb black Hamburgh ½ lb sweet-water	2 lb black Hamburgh ½ lb sweet-water	2 lb Black Prince 1 lb muscadine	2 lb Black Prince 1 lb muscadine
Small salad	1 pint	1 pint	½ pint	¾ pint
Cucumbers	2 brace	4 brace	6 brace	4 brace

The items being filled into the table, the next thing is to copy off on a slip of paper, the names and quantities of the articles sent, which paper is delivered as a bill of parcels by the man with the donkey-cart to the clerk of the kitchen.

A similar plan is pursued in some other great places; but, instead of entering them in a table, they are entered in a journal, which is sent to the kitchen along with the articles, and brought back again to the gardener. If nothing is said or written by the clerk or cook, it is concluded that every thing entered for that day has been received safe, and is of a satisfactory quality.

We found the open garden excellently cropped with large supplies of those standard articles of winter consumption, broccoli, celery, and endive. In the houses was a large supply of retarded black and white grapes, pine-apples that promised a succession during the whole winter, and a fig-house in full crop. No attention seemed any where to be paid to neatness or orderly keeping; but every effort to the production of excellent crops.

The pleasure-grounds at Ashridge Park are under a separate direction from the kitchen-garden: the gardener was, when we visited them, Mr. Poynter, formerly propagator in Messrs. Colvill's nursery. He had every thing in very high order and keeping, and especially the plants in two large conservatories.

The pleasure-grounds here extend in front of the house, without being continued either to the right or left of it, as in most instances of successful effect in pleasure-ground scenery.

There is a small spot, surrounded by a hedge of box, called the Monk's Garden; another, called the French Garden; a rosary, rockwork, and some other separate scenes; the

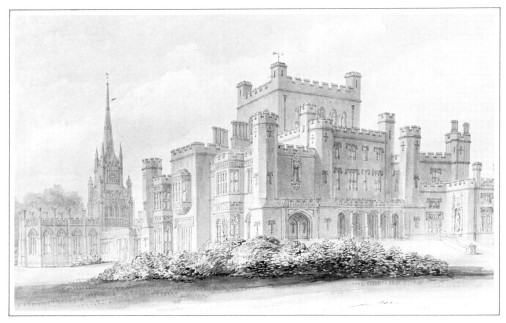

ASHRIDGE PARK — 'THIS GRAND AND IRREGULAR PILE IS SEEN TO VERY GOOD ADVANTAGE.'

ASHRIDGE PARK, CONSERVATORY.

best of which is the rockwork, composed of large masses of plum-pudding stone, a production which abounds in this county. There is no great variety of plants in the conservatories; but such as there are, in general of the most showy kinds; and, being brought forward in reserve-houses, are only placed in the conservatory when in flower, or in their best state. The principal conservatory connects the state-rooms with the chapel; and, we should think, is one of the finest Gothic structures for plants in England. (We have since seen that at Alton Towers, in Staffordshire, which is considerably larger, and when we last saw it, in 1831, was in the very best possible order.)

The surface of the park is not without considerable undulations; but these are not heightened or brought into effect in a picturesque point of view by the emplacement of the wood. There is, also, a total want of water. To make the park what it ought to be, in correspondence with the house, water ought to be brought by a steam engine and iron pipes from the nearest practicable stream, and the valley to the left of the house flooded. The approach from Dunstable would then pass over a bridge; and the pleasure-ground might be narrowed opposite the house, and extended along the margin of this lake, or river, to any extent and with variations in the distant scenery, which our hasty glance did not enable us to determine. In short, while the highest degree of art and expense has been displayed on the house, scarcely anything has been done to the grounds to render them a worthy accompaniment to such a splendid pile.

WOBURN ABBEY

OCTOBER 15. WOBURN ABBEY. — Went round the park with Mr. Forbes, the gardener, venerating that fine old drive through evergreens, said to have been planted by Miller. The dark green hollies, with trunks of timber size, with their shining leaves and coral berries, remind us of the time of Evelyn, and his fine hedge at Sayes Court, which the Czar Peter made gaps in, by having himself wheeled through it by his attendants.

We turned out of the drive to the thornery, a most picturesque morceau of huge and fantastic oaks, grotesque old thorns, hazels, and dogwoods; on ground abruptly varied, and appropriated to man and elegant enjoyment, by a highly characteristic cottage with a Scotch kitchen and furniture.

There are a number of ornamental cottages scattered round the margin of Woburn park, of much exterior beauty, with neat gardens, kept in good order under the direction of the head gardener. In most of them is an apartment for the reception of small parties from the Abbey, who wish to amuse themselves by allusions to primitive simplicity: for it is one of the enjoyments of those who are habituated to live in a style of high art and refinement, to take

occasional refuge in the contrast produced by comparative artlessness and simplicity.

OCTOBER 16. This, being Monday, is the public day for seeing through the house and pleasure-grounds at Woburn Abbey. Of the house, and the building connected with it, we shall only observe that the gallery of statuary is the most extraordinary thing of the kind in Britain, out of London. It is gratifying, in another gallery, in the interior of the Abbey, to observe the models of cattle and other domestic animals reared under the direction of the late Duke Francis. In one room is a series of miniatures of the heads of the Russell family, from the earliest times to the present. A biographical account of them has been written by the late Mr. Wiffen (whose lamented death we have heard of while passing this sheet through the press.).

The pleasure-ground is a large roundish area behind the Abbey. There are a few fine old specimens in it of oaks, pines, firs, and cedars, but very few rare trees or shrubs. Since the accession of the present duke, it has been very greatly improved in one small spot near the house. Some beautiful flower-gardens have been formed from the designs of Repton, and the suggestions of the present duchess; but the principal features are the exotic and hardy heatheries, formed under the particular direction of the duke. A willow-ground is in contemplation, which will be a great addition to the interest of the scenery. We must not forget the grass-garden, the most complete thing of the kind which has ever been formed in any country.

OCTOBER 17. WOBURN TO HATFIELD. Hatfield House, the residence of the Marquess of Salisbury, is in the Elizabethan style, and deservedly celebrated. The park is extensive, but

HATFIELD HOUSE, — IN THE ELIZABETHAN STYLE, AND DESERVEDLY
CELEBRATED.

not remarkably interesting; and the gardens afford little to gratify the amateur. There is an antique flower-garden, with walks arched over with clipped lime trees, which is separated from the house by a terrace-walk of turf. Beyond this garden is another, also devoted to flowers, and containing a range of hot-houses, for the culture of pine-apples and grapes. The kitchen-garden is in a different and distinct part of the grounds. The whole is very well kept; but there are no rare plants, either hardy or exotic; and there is but little evidence of such a love of gardening in the proprietor, as would be sufficient to stimulate and encourage his gardener.

HATFIELD HOUSE, IN THE GROUNDS.

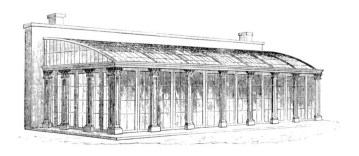

5

A TOUR FROM

TO

SHEFFIELD

MAY 1839

Though notices of more than one of our tours have been left unfinished, yet, before we resume them, we shall devote a few pages to some recollections of what we saw during a late excursion. Having been called professionally into Derbyshire, we went to Birmingham by the railway, and thence to Derby and Sheffield. At the latter town we saw the botanic garden and the general cemetery, and in its neighbourhood Chatsworth; and near Derby we saw the different residences of the Messrs. Strutt, and also Bretby Hall, Keddlestone Hall, Elvaston Castle, &c.

TREES are the objects which have most effect in improving the natural features of a country, and therefore we begin with them. Many belts of plantation, particularly in Derbyshire, which were newly planted, or made but very little appearance, in 1806, are now from 50ft. to 70ft. in height, and have completely changed the face of the country. The black Italian poplar (Populus monilifera) in 1806 was little known, but was strongly recommended by the Messrs. Pontey of Huddersfield, and planted very generally throughout the north of England. In 1826, these poplars began to take the lead of all the other trees in plantations made during the first ten years of the present century: while at present (1839) they are conspicuous in every part of the country, and have completely overtopped the old oaks, and in many cases even the elms. In 1806, the only poplars that were to be seen of any size were, the white poplar, and the common black poplar, with occasionally a Lombardy poplar, rearing its cypress-like head in some gentlemen's pleasure-grounds; but now these and all other poplars are lost amid the multiplicity of the trees of the black Italian kind.

The great objection to these trees is the sameness which they produce in the appearance of the landscape; but this sameness is greatly owing to all the trees being apparently of similar forms, ages, and sizes; conditions that will be changed as soon as a part of the trees become fully grown, and are partially cut down as timber. Why should they be objected to merely because they do not satisfy the eye that looks at them with reference only to one particular kind of beauty or effect? Artists, from the time of Gilpin, have, in our opinion, been far too exclusive in their mode of viewing nature; and, by confining their admiration to the picturesque or sculpturesque, or, in other words, to what is peculiarly suitable for their art, they have lost sight of the beauties of high polish, neatness, cultivation, agriculture, architecture, arboriculture, and other kinds far more important to society, and affording much greater evidence of civilisation, comfort, and the general diffusion of human happiness, than mere picturesque beauty.

FARMING. — On the surface of the farm lands, throughout the tract in question, with the exception of those parts where commons have been enclosed, there is, perhaps, no great change recognisable at a distance. The surfaces of moist meadows are still, at this season, yellow with the blossoms of the crowfoot, an indication that they are not sufficiently drained; and the dry gravelly surface of grass lands about Lichfield and Shenstone are, at this season, white with the downy seeds of the dandelion, a proof that they have not been sufficiently manured, or clayed; or sown down with such grasses and clovers as will form a thick matting on the surface, and subdue, and ultimately starve out, the dandelion. As to agricultural practices from London to Derby, the clumsiest forms of ploughs may still be seen, drawn with from three to five horses in a line, at a snail's pace; and on gravelly soils, preparing for turnips, more especially in the neighbourhood of Shenstone, the heaps of couchgrass ready to be burned, are as thick as the heaps of dung ready to be spread abroad should be. In short, we saw such very bad farming in the neighbourhood of Lichfield and Shenstone, that it is difficult to conceive how the farmers can pay any rent worth mentioning, and live comfortably.

THE TOWNS, it is almost unnecessary to say, have been wonderfully improved since 1806, and the progress of Birmingham, even since 1831, when we last saw it, is astonishing. We shall confine ourselves to noticing the great increase in the number of the villas, in that part of the neighbourhood of Birmingham which surrounds the botanic garden. There is a great improvement in their exterior architecture, and more choice plants are conspicuous in their gardens. The botanic garden has already had a considerable effect in improving the general taste of the Birmingham people for plants. Very little change has taken place in Lichfield, as it is neither a place of commerce nor of manufacture; but the little town of Walsall exhibits some very handsome small villas and street houses, erected within the last seven years, which are not surpassed by any suburban villas in the neighbourhood of London. Dudley has had the approach from Birmingham widened; but we were sorry to hear, when in this town, that the lime-works are being extended under the old castle in such a manner, that the fall of that venerable and picturesque group of ruins is anticipated by the townspeople. The park at Himley is undergoing the same subterranean operations, and the noble mansion there, it is said, will, in all probability, be pulled down in consequence. Derby has improved rapidly. There are now building, an athenæum, post-office, banking-house and hotel, which will form a splendid continuous elevation. But what, perhaps, was more gratifying than anything else that we saw during the whole of our tour, was the marked improvement that we observed in the construction of the roadside cottages, wherever any had been recently built; and the greater display of fine flowers in the front gardens, both of new and old cottages. There is hardly one of these gardens that does not contain some of the fine plants sent home by Douglas and Drummond, or plants of Mexico and South America.

RAILROADS. — We say nothing of the railroads going forward everywhere, or the magnificent bridges that would lead us out of our province. We cannot, however, help expressing our admiration at the science exhibited in these works, and especially in the bridges of the

RAILROADS – 'WE CANNOT...HELP EXPRESSING OUR ADMIRATION AT THE SCIENCE EXHIBITED IN THESE WORKS, AND ESPECIALLY IN THE BRIDGES OF THE LONDON AND BIRMINGHAM RAILWAY.'

London and Birmingham railway, even as seen during a rapid transit beneath them. The stupendous cuttings in some places, the high embankments in others, the lofty bridges crossing the road every now and then, the tunnels in which all is darkness, and the beautiful and extensive views from the embankments and viaducts, render this road, which hypothetically might be considered dull and monotonous, actually full of variety.

GRATUITIES TO SERVANTS AT SHOW HOUSES. — Among other changes which have taken place since 1806, we may notice the difference in the gratuities given to servants for showing great houses. At that time, few persons, after being shown through such houses at Chatsworth, Bretby Hall, Wentworth House, &c. thought of giving less than gold; but now 5*s.*, and even 2*s. 6d.*, are received with thanks. We wish a similar reform could be made in the gratuities given to coachmen, guards, the drivers of post-chaises, and waiters. With respect to show houses, we sometimes think it would be an improvement, for every proprietor who had a show house to have a fixed sum per head for showing it on certain days, say to travellers; and to show it on certain other days, which may be supposed to be those in which the poorer persons of the neighbourhood will come, for nothing. However, it is much better that the houses of men of wealth and taste should be shown, even for a considerable sum, than not shown at all; because such exhibitions cannot fail to have some influence in improving the taste of the spectators, and showing the wealthy tradesman or manufacturer what he may aspire to.

KEDDLESTON HALL; THE EARL OF SCARSDALE. — This noble place is well known for its superb mansion of classical architecture, its hall of lofty columns of native marble, and its gigantic timber trees. There is very little about Keddleston that we could wish to add to, or alter. We

KEDDLESTON HALL – 'WELL KNOWN FOR ITS SUPERB MANSION OF CLASSICAL ARCHITECTURE, ITS HALL OF LOFTY COLUMNS OF NATIVE MARBLE, AND ITS GIGANTIC TIMBER TREES.'

examined the lofty silver firs in the pleasure-ground, varying from 100ft. to 130ft., or perhaps 150ft. in height; and the large oaks, and broad-leaved elms in the park. The plantation on the hill behind the house, however, from not being thinned in time, admits the light through the naked stems, and thus has a meagre, instead of a massive effect. An attempt is making to plant out the stable offices, which, if it succeed, will, in our opinion, injure the general appearance of the house; the dignity and effect of which they at present heighten by forming a secondary mass. We found in the pleasure-grounds specimens of laurustinus from 6ft. to 8ft. in height, and as much in diameter, and large arbutuses, and common and Portugal laurels, which had been but slightly, if at all, injured by the winter of 1837-8.

CHATSWORTH; HIS GRACE THE DUKE OF DEVONSHIRE. — Since we last saw this place in 1831, it has undergone many improvements, and of these the most remarkable is the erection of a large tropical conservatory. In general design it may be compared to a cathedral with a central aile and side ailes. The entrances will be at the ends, through porches, which will be treated as green-houses; and, when the whole is completed, it will cover above an acre and a quarter of ground. There will be a carriage drive through it; which will form part of a general drive through the pleasure-grounds. The conservatory is situated in an open part of a lofty wood, in nearly the centre of the pleasure-grounds, and it is unquestionably the largest structure of the kind in existence or on record. The framework of the main building, which is of wood, is all put up, and is just beginning to be glazed. It will be heated by six fires, all of which, and the means of access to them, the places for fuel, &c., will be under ground, and the chimneys carried in a tunnel up the side of a hill to the distance of nearly a furlong, so that not the slightest appearance of artificial heating, or smoke, or sheds, &c. will appear, either within the house or exterior to it. We shall not enter into details, because, when the building is finished, these will doubtless be made public by Mr. Paxton; by whom the whole has been designed, and under whose direction it has been executed. We cannot avoid noticing the very judicious manner in which Mr. Paxton has proceeded with this building, which will be

CHATSWORTH – 'SINCE LAST WE SAW THIS PLACE IN 1831,
IT HAS UNDERGONE MANY IMPROVEMENTS ...'

CHATSWORTH – 'THE CONSERVATORY IS SITUATED IN AN OPEN PART OF A
LOFTY WOOD, IN NEARLY THE CENTRE OF THE PLEASURE-GROUNDS AND IT IS
UNQUESTIONABLY THE LARGEST STRUCTURE OF THE KIND IN EXISTENCE OR
ON RECORD.'

completed in the most scientific, elegant, and substantial manner; and with a degree of
economy, considering the immense magnitude of the structure, that will in the end surprise
every one and redound greatly to his credit, and to the honour of the noble duke, his
benevolent and enlightened employer.

The arboretum at Chatsworth, is the only one that we have seen or heard of where
sufficient room is given to every species to attain its usual size. The trees and shrubs have now
been planted four years, and they may be considered as firmly established, and doing well.
Each tree and larger-growing shrub is planted on a little hill, the surface of which is kept dug,
or at all events free from weeds, which is perhaps better; and the smaller-growing shrubs,

180

CHATSWORTH – 'THE TERMINATION OF THE SLOPING LINE OF THE CASCADE
HAS, LIKE THAT AT CASERTA NEAR NAPLES, ALWAYS APPEARED TO US
UNSATISFACTORY; THOUGH IT WOULD BE DIFFICULT TO SAY, BOTH IN THE
CASE OF CASERTA AND CHATSWORTH, WHAT WOULD BE THE BEST MODE OF
IMPROVING IT.'

such as heath, azaleas, vacciniums, &c., are planted in masses in prepared soil kept free from weeds. An ample space is allowed to each plant; the effect of which, now that they are fairly beginning to grow, is already conspicuous, and will be strikingly so in five or six years. The names are in white letters on a dark ground painted on heart of oak; but the letters are beginning to fade, and will be replaced by others of a different kind, and more in the manner of our brick tally. Near the palace, as it may very properly be termed, many araucarias and deodar cedars are planted, alternating with Portugal laurels trained on stems 6ft. high, with heads cut into round balls, so as to resemble orange trees under the kind of treatment which they receive in the gardens of the Tuileries and at Versailles. A new line of separation has been formed between the pleasure-ground and the park, on the east side, which is a very great improvement. It is a high wall rising in steps as it ascends the hill, and the space between each step is thrown into a compartment by piers. Each compartment is planted with tender climbers, or other ornamental shrubs, which are trained to a trellis, and covered with a blue striped canvass curtain during nights throughout the winter and spring. During the three or four summer months, the curtain is entirely removed. This conservative wall, as it may be called, commences at the orangery, which forms part of the palace, and terminates in a stove at some distance. In this stove we found many well grown plants; and, in particular, groups of ferns on masses of rockwork, each mass being placed behind the stone piers between the windows of the front elevation. The grand cascade has been altered, but something further is wanting; the fall of the water from the aqueduct not harmonising in breadth either with the falls above or those below it. The termination of the sloping line of cascade has, like that at Caserta near Naples, always appeared to us unsatisfactory; though it would be difficult to say, both in the case of Caserta and Chatsworth, what would be the best mode of improving it. Mr. Paxton, however, having recently had the advantage, during an eight months' tour with his noble employer, of visiting all the finest gardens of France and Italy (an advantage which we question whether any other gardener ever enjoyed), will doubtless devise some plan for giving meaning, not only to the termination of the line of cascades, but to the two ends of the oblong canal on the south front of the house.

Perhaps the most important improvement which Mr. Paxton has introduced at Chatsworth is, the mode of ridge and furrow roofing which he has adopted in hot-house building. Some idea may be formed of this from two sashes figured in the first edition of our *Encyclopædia of Gardening*, and also from the description of the ridge and furrow roof given in the same volume; and in our *Remarks on Hothouses*, 4to, published in 1816.

ELVASTON CASTLE; THE SEAT OF THE EARL OF HARRINGTON. — We had frequently heard this place described as a modern Palagonia, and we knew that it contained an excellent collection of the pine and fir tribe, and also of Cupressinæ and Taxaceæ. We were therefore most anxious to see it, and, through the kindness of the proprietor, our wishes have been gratified. The situation is flat, or at least without any striking inequalities; but there are some fine old avenues, one of which is nearly a mile and a half in length, but the effect is that of an avenue of ten miles, in consequence of the ground beyond falling below the level of the surface where the avenue commences at the house. Upwards of seven years ago all the trees and hedges were cleared away for nearly seven miles, which came in the line, and the view is now uninterrupted until the eye rests upon the hills in Nottinghamshire, at the distance of ten miles. The effect of these avenues has been heightened in an extraordinary degree, by the formation of new ones, chiefly of the upright or Irish yew. Two of these avenues, one upwards of 750ft. in length, and 60ft. in breadth, and the other 800ft. in length, are planted, first, with upright yews, and next with red cedars; with a third or back row, on each side of the avenue, of deodar cedars grafted on the cedar of Lebanon. All these plants are thriving luxuriantly, and their effect will be striking in a very few years. Beyond one of these avenues, in a space occupying several acres, is an extensive collection of pines on the outside of a corresponding avenue.

The castle is a magnificent building externally; and the interior contains some spacious apartments, well arranged, and richly furnished and fitted up, with curious carving, gilding, stained glass, pictures, and sculptures. The offices are very complete, and the kitchen, the dairy, and the larder, are particularly deserving of notice; the latter is a lofty tower, placed over the ice-house.

The kitchen-garden is large, and it contains some new forcing-houses, admirably planned and executed, and furnished with excellent crops of pines, grapes, and peaches. The front borders for the vines are covered during winter with tiles cemented with clay, so as completely to carry off the rain and melting snow to a drain in front. These tiles are annually taken off in May, and put on again in December. The peach borders are about 6ft. in width, and 18 in. in depth; with the bottom paved with tiles, to prevent the roots from entering the subsoil; and the surface covered with tiles, to prevent evaporation, to conduct heat to the soil,

ELVASTON CASTLE, – 'THE CASTLE IS A MAGNIFICENT BUILDING EXTERNALLY.'

and to reflect it to the foliage against the walls. In general, all the fruit trees, both standards and dwarfs in the open garden, and trees against the walls, have a flooring of tiles under the roots, from 1ft. to 18in. beneath the surface. These tiles are made 1ft. square, and 1¼in. thick. The crops on these trees, and the moderate state of the wood, neither too luxuriant nor too weak, prove the great advantages of the plan. Indeed, we attach so much importance to it, that we should wish much to lay Mr. Barron's practice and opinions on this point of culture before our readers. The system of covering with tiles also deserves the particular attention of the gardener. We have seldom seen such an elegant range of glass, covering plants so beautifully grown, and bearing so abundantly, as this garden contains.

Among single objects which we recall to memory are, purple beeches grafted at a great height on the common beech; a weeping ash grafted on a common ash at 80ft. from the ground, and growing most luxuriantly; and many variegated yews. A drive has recently been formed round the plantations in connexion with the pleasure-grounds, about two miles in length; the ground on each side, to a considerable width has been trenched, and will be planted with evergreen trees or shrubs of a similar description to those already there.

On the whole, the grounds at Elvaston Castle abound with objects of great singularity, rarity, and value, and we can only regret our utter inability to do them justice, though our visit occupied the greater part of the day. Unfortunately, Mr. Barron, the gardener, was from home, and we were shown round by a young man who was comparatively a stranger. We trust, however, to Mr. Barron to supply deficiencies, and correct any mistake into which we may have fallen; and, above all, to give us some account of the manner in which he transplants large trees, and paves under and otherwise manages the fruit trees in the kitchen-garden.

ELVASTON CASTLE – 'ON THE WHOLE THE GROUNDS AT ELVASTON CASTLE
ABOUND WITH OBJECTS OF GREAT SINGULARITY, RARITY AND VALUE, AND WE
CAN ONLY REGRET OUR UTTER INABILITY TO DO THEM JUSTICE, THOUGH OUR
VISIT OCCUPIED THE GREATER PART OF THE DAY.'

ELVASTON CASTLE – BIRDS EYE VIEW OF MON PLAISIR DETAIL

185

AMBRA GARDEN

ELVASTON CASTLE – BIRDS EYE VIEW OF MON PLAISIR DETAIL

6

A TOUR IN

LINCOLNSHIRE,

AND

STAFFORDSHIRE

MAY 1840

HARLAXTON MANOR.—MAY 20. We had heard much of this place from various architects and amateurs for several years; and an accidental circumstance having brought us in communication with its proprietor, Gregory Gregory, Esq., that gentleman kindly acceded to our wish to see the works going forward on the new site chosen by him for the family residence. Mr. Gregory resides at Hungerton Hall, about five miles from Grantham, and his building and gardening operations are carrying on in a striking situation on the side of the hill, between Hungerton and Grantham, near the ancient village of Harlaxton, as well as in that village. The improvements consist of the erection of a large mansion in the style of James I., the laying out of gardens around it in the geometric style, and the picturesque decoration of the village. As Mr. Gregory superintends every part of these improvements very much himself, both as respects the design and detail, he has been obliged to confine the admission to these works, during their progress, to his own immediate acquaintance; both for the comfort of his own privacy, and on account of the disadvantages that would arise from the interruption of successive visitors.

The grandfather of the present proprietor married the heiress of a branch of the noble family of De Ligne, subsequently to its alliance with that of the Dukes d'Arenberg. Our readers will remember that it was the celebrated Prince de Ligne, chief of this family, who was so conspicuous in the leading royal courts of Europe, at the close of the last century, from his sparkling wit and talents; and that he, owing to his extensive travels, was the first who was enabled to publish a general view of the style, feeling, and taste of gardens throughout Europe, and who created those of his own family seat at Beloeil, in Hainault, which are mentioned in the poem of *Les Jardins* by De Lille:—

"Beloeil tout a la fois magnifique et champetre."

Harlaxton was purchased at the end of the fifteenth century by a younger branch of this family, who, having embraced the reformed religion, came to England to avoid the persecutions of the Duke of Alva, in the time of Philip of Spain. They brought with them great wealth, and made those alterations in the mansion-house which are of the period of James I., and contribute so much to give it the present striking appearance. The family portraits, and the arms of the family in stained glass, with a pedigree written in the French language of the day, are still preserved in the house. It is an interesting family record, showing how many of this house have been knights of the Golden Fleece, and borne many important charges of government, both civil and military, during so long a period in the annals of the Low Countries and the empire.

Mr. Gregory, having determined to build a new family mansion, informs us that he studied the subject for several years previous to commencing it. He visited almost every part of Europe, and part of Asia; and, having determined to adopt the style of James I., and there being, at the time he commenced, in 1822, few or no books on the subject, he examined personally most of the houses in Britain in that style, or bearing a close analogy to it. He also found that the buildings of the two universities exhibited much of domestic purpose in style and character.

The main body of the house is quadrangular, and it is placed on the only true principle for the climate of Britain; viz, that of having an imaginary line from north to south to form the diagonal of a square. The main approach will be straight, and very nearly a mile in length. From the public road it first gradually descends more than half its length to the bottom of a valley, in which a lake of great extent might readily be formed; and then it as gradually ascends to the court of honour in front of the mansion.

Of the different elevations, we can only say that they are exquisitely rich and beautiful. The frontispiece over the entrance-portal, the general form of which resembles that at Northumberland House, has rich accompaniments of the inscription and date of building, and its founder, in pierced stone, of finer character and dimensions than those of Castle Ashby or Temple Newsham. The elevation of a part of the private family apartments in the drawingroom front is quite an architectural gem. The central bell-tower, and the angular turrets, all roofed with stone, produce ideas of grandeur and durability intensely felt, but not readily to be described. The value of everything, indeed, is enhanced by the substantialness of the materials, and the excellence of the workmanship.

The terraced gardens will be on seven different levels, communicating by flights of steps, ornamented with vases, figures, and numerous other suitable objects; and, in appropriate places, there will be canals, basins, and fountains, summer-houses, shrubs clipped into artificial forms, &c. The upper terrace will be 150ft. higher than the house, and will form a winding plateau, extending along the ridge of the hill on which the house stands, and commanding, on one side, a very rich view over a fine agricultural and wooded district, and, on the other, the mountains of Derbyshire, forty miles distant. The two extremities of the terrace-gardens will gradually be united to broad walks on the same levels as the terraces, in

HARLAXTON MANOR – 'THE CENTRAL BELL-TOWER AND THE ANGULAR
TURRETS, ALL ROOFED WITH STONE PRODUCE IDEAS OF GRANDEUR AND
DURABILITY INTENSELY FELT, BUT NOT READILY TO BE DESCRIBED.'

HARLAXTON MANOR

extensive woods already existing. After these walks have been continued to a certain length on the same level as the terraces, the upper one will gradually descend, and the lower one gradually rise, till, at a considerable distance from the house, they will form, by gentle inclined planes, communications with every level of walk or terrace. At least, the situation admits of this kind of arrangement, as well as of several others.

One thing is however certain, that Mr. Gregory will create what may be called an atmosphere of highly artificial garden scenery in the geometric style, round and overhanging the mansion; and that he will gradually unite it, not with modern shrubbery walks, but with the picturesque woods already existing, harmonising these woods with the artificial scenery by the introduction of foreign plants. For ornamenting the geometric garden, Mr. Gregory possesses an ample stock of vases, statues, and other sculptural ornaments, and of rich gates, and other iron work, collected by him on all parts of the Continent, soon after the peace of 1815.

In the natural woods at Harlaxton, Mr. Gregory has introduced masses of rhodo-dendrons, holly, periwinkle, tutsan, laurel, and other evergreen shrubs; and a great many sorts of herbaceous plants, including bulbs and Californian annuals. One interesting circum-

192

HARLAXTON MANOR, THE KITCHEN GARDEN.

stance we cannot avoid mentioning, which is, that when Mr. Gregory was travelling in the Caucasus, and also in the Crimea, he saw the Heracleum giganteum, and thinking it a very suitable plant for the Harlaxton woods, and not knowing that it was already introduced into England, he had a young plant taken up, planted in a box, and sent from Constantinople to England. This plant has left a numerous progeny, which are now luxuriating in a favourite spot called the Cimetière, in the woods at Harlaxton.

BELTON, NEAR GRANTHAM; EARL BROWNLOW.—MAY 21. We passed to this place from Harlaxton, through Grantham, and a very miserable village, which we could not help wishing had belonged to Mr. Gregory. The wretched hovels exhibited not only a want of taste in their exteriors and surrounding gardens, but even a want of repair and the appearance of common comforts. Belton we have always understood to be one of the best kept places in England, and we certainly found it so, though the family had been absent some months, and were not expected till July. The grounds have few natural inequalities; but the river Witham runs through them, and this feature has been made the most of, especially near the house, which is a fine old French mansion, with stately avenues. Among the old trees are some good specimens, especially of elm and Scotch pine. There is a rustic bridge leading over a piece of

BELTON – 'BELTON WE HAVE ALWAYS UNDERSTOOD TO BE ONE OF THE BEST
KEPT PLACES IN ENGLAND, AND WE CERTAINLY FOUND IT SO, THOUGH THE
FAMILY HAD BEEN ABSENT SOME MONTHS.'

water to what may be called a fancy cottage, which is covered over with rustic trelliswork for
climbers, and these climbers are planted in rustic boxes, which project from the outside of the
parapet of the bridge. The idea is comparatively new, and the effect good. In the church, the
tower of which forms a fine object from the walk in the pleasure-grounds which leads to it,
are some fine sculptural monuments of the Brownlow family, and in the churchyard are
several to their servants; kindness and consideration to them being apparently hereditary in
the family. One tombstone is to the memory of a gardener, who had been 54 years in the
family, and died in 1710. The place has two defects which might easily be remedied. The first
is, that there is no master walk so conducted as to display the main features of the place; and
the second, that the kitchen-garden cannot be entered without crossing a public road, and
also, if we are not mistaken, a farm road. A tunnel or tunnels would at once remove the latter
objection, and facilitate the removal of the former.

The home farm–offices are very complete; we entered the poultry-house, which is a
square room, well lighted, and heated by an open fireplace. There is a range round the room
of coops for hens with chickens; above it, one for laying-hens; and above that, one for such as
are hatching. On each side a hen stair leads to the roosting-place, which is above the ceiling,
so that nothing can ever drop on the floor. The village here is being remodeled in the Gothic
style in good taste, and is already a most gratifying and conspicuous ornament to the public

road. Would that His Lordship might extend this admirable improvement to all the cottages on the estate! By way of expression of purpose, the smithy has a large horseshoe sculptured on the gable, which projects over the entrance. The inn and public houses have carved stone figures for their signs; the beautiful schoolhouse has a quotation, and the village shop has a riband label of of stone (too broad, and not very tastefully displayed) over the broad window for displaying the goods. In the flower-garden we observed a curious hybrid between a Brompton stock and a wallflower, which appeared to be producing seed; and which, at all events, we trust Mr. Ingram has propagated by cuttings.

Chatsworth.—May 23. When we last visited this place in May, 1839, the grand conservatory was just beginning to be glazed, and at present the glazing is almost completed. Perhaps the operations that we were most gratified with, on our present visit to Chatsworth, were those carrying on in the village of Edensor. The cottages are being rebuilt, added to, or repaired and ornamented, and their gardens will be enlarged and tastefully laid out and planted. All the houses will be supplied with water from an elevated source, the village being on the side of a hill; and there will be a public play-ground and open shed, and a public drying-ground. Behind the houses are the fields for grazing the cows, of which each cottager has one or more. The school is almost the only building so far finished as to enable us to judge of its effect, which, we think, will be excellent. We entered several of the cottages, and found them most comfortable and commodious within; all of them had back kitchens, pantries, and dairies for the produce of the cow, with the sleeping-rooms up stairs. We have no doubt, that, when this village is completed according to Mr. Paxton's ideas, His Grace the Duke will be so much pleased with it, as to cause a revision to be made of all the cottages on his extensive estates; and a better mode of doing good, both positively to the occupants, and by

CHATSWORTH.

example, to the cottagers of other proprietors, and to cottagers generally, we do not think could be devised.

All that Derbyshire wants, to render it the most beautiful and interesting county in England, is, plantations on the high grounds to improve the climate and beautify the face of the country, and more artistical cottages, farmhouses, and gardens.

CHATSWORTH TO WOOTTON LODGE, BY CHESTERFIELD AND DERBY.—MAY 24. To Chesterfield the country is bleak, but the fields are divided by stone walls, and tolerably well cultivated. The railroad from Chesterfield to Derby passes through the most interesting tract of country on the line between Sheffield and London; and the road from Derby, by Ashbourne to Alton Towers, is most romantic.

WOOTTON LODGE is a remarkably fine old place. The house is a square building, of the time of Elizabeth, imposing from the magnitude of the mass, and from its great height, considering, that it is a dwelling-house, in proportion to its width. It is situated on a prominent rock or hill, surrounded on three sides by a deep ravine, which separates it from higher hills, which are covered with oak woods. The elevation of the house, we repeat, is very imposing, and this arises chiefly from magnitude, and from the height and breadth of the many mullioned windows, and the large spaces of naked wall between them.

Altogether, the exterior of this house deserves the study of the architect, not for its ornaments or details, for these are few, but to find out the cause of the powerful impression which it makes on the mind. We were not within, but from the large windows and the broad space between them in the elevation, it is impossible to doubt, that the interior contains some very magnificent rooms. It is entered through a court of honour, with offices as wings or lodges to the right and left of the entrance to the court; and beyond these, on the steep sides of the hill, are the terraced gardens and walks among the rocks and aged yew trees which surround the house, except on the entrance side. On a platform facing one of the fronts, there is a curious raised garden, with a canal bordered with masonry, and containing a fountain in

WOOTTON LODGE – 'IT IS SITUATED ON A PROMINENT ROCK OR HILL
SURROUNDED ON THREE SIDES BY A DEEP RAVINE WHICH SEPARATES IT FROM
OTHER HILLS WHICH ARE COVERED IN OAK WOODS.'

NEAR TRENTHAM HALL

IN STAFFORDSHIRE

the form of a duck, doubtless coeval with the building. Near the kitchen entrance we observed, against the wall, a case of about 4ft., containing an overshot water-wheel, supplied by a ½in. pipe of water used for turning the roasting-jack. It is impossible, as it seems to us, not to be charmed with this place.

ALTON TOWERS.—We had only time to take a hasty glance at what may be called the enchanted valley, and to see a new flower-garden recently tastefully designed and most scientifically laid out by Mr. Forsyth, in one of the courts of the Abbey. The valley, in the time of the late Lord Shrewsbury, had a peculiar charm, from the great number of objects, all of an artificial and singular or grotesque character, in so romantic a situation, and from the trees and shrubs being either small, or cut or clipped into artificial shapes.

ALTON TOWERS – 'WE ONLY HAD TIME TO TAKE A HASTY GLANCE AT WHAT
MAY BE CALLED THE ENCHANTED VALLEY.'

TRENTHAM HALL.—MAY 25. The road from Alton Towers, by Cheadle, is at first hilly and romantic, and afterwards rich and varied. The alterations and additions to the house at Trentham are far advanced, and they have had a magical effect on the place. The effect of the tower at one angle, in forming a centre to the general mass, carrying it off, as artists say, or, in artistical philosophy, communicating an axis of symmetry, is most satisfactory. The central tower at Alton Towers is too small for the immense pile of buildings that surround it, having been built, no doubt, before it was contemplated to increase them to such an extent; but this at Trentham appears of the proper dimensions, unless, perhaps, it is not sufficiently high. The first or upper flower-garden is laid out in what the French call the English style, with beds of turf, and dug beds edged with box or gravel, and has an excellent effect, the whole forming a raised platform edged with stone. The lower or main garden has the leading walks formed and gravelled, and the slopes turfed; but, not being yet planted, it has rather a naked appearance. We were shown some Portugal laurels, which were training with clean stems and round heads, to imitate the orange trees of the Continent, as at Chatsworth, to be planted along the main walks at regular distances in stone boxes. If the Portugal laurels were budded

TRENTHAM HALL – 'THE ALTERATIONS AND ADDITIONS TO THE HOUSE...ARE FAR ADVANCED, AND THEY HAVE HAD A MAGICAL EFFECT ON THE PLACE.'

standard high with the common laurel, the effect would be still more striking, as the light green of the leaves would render the allusion to the orange tree much more complete. Such imitations of orange trees are not uncommon in the neighbourhood of Paris, where the laurel is grafted standard high on the common cherry, which, however, being a deciduous plant, does not form so good a stock for an evergreen as the Portugal laurel would. The common laurel, to a general observer, is so very like the orange, that, some years ago, a foreign ambassador, who was going round the grounds at Claremont with the gardener, Mr. McIntosh, took the laurel undergrowths there, with which the woods abound, for dwarf orange trees, and expressed his astonishment at seeing the orange thrive so well in England.

TRENTHAM HALL, THE TERRACE.

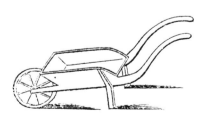

TRENTHAM HALL, THE TERRACE.

7

A TOUR IN

SCOTLAND

JULY – AUGUST 1841

GARSCUBE, SIR ARCHIBALD CAMPBELL, BART. — Imagine a broad extensive basin of park scenery, bounded on two sides by irregular banks finely wooded, and the two ends lost by the banks apparently closing on a noble river with a rocky bottom and sides. Such is the idea that we formed of Garscube, when first we emerged from the fine old wood which covers an approach conducted down one of the steep banks. The effect is striking, from the surface of the ground, and the manner in which it is entered from the public road. After turning to the right, and while the imagination is still at work, we are whirled down for a considerable distance, till, at the base of the slope, we emerge into a beautifully undulated park, containing a splendid river, close to which we see the house, in the domestic Gothic style of Mr. Burns. Having crossed a handsome and well placed bridge, we arrive at the porch, and soon enter the house by one step; but it struck us at the time that three steps would have given more dignity to the views from the apartments within, as well as the idea of a greater degree of

GARSCUBE – 'THE PLACE WAS MODERATELY WELL KEPT, PARTICULARLY THE
KITCHEN GARDEN, AND THOUGH IT RAINED THE WHOLE TIME THAT WE WERE
VIEWING IT, WE LEFT IT VERY MUCH DELIGHTED.'

security from damp to the stranger entering from without. The apartments seemed well arranged; and the conservatory had a noble effect, from the splendid irregularity of the masses of leaves and flowers which over-arched the paths, and clothed the back wall with a surface of vegetation, from which many branches protruded.

We could refer to many conservatories in England, where, from allowing every plant to assume its native vigour, and occupy whatever bulk it can in the house, the whole surface of the glass comes at last to be covered with, perhaps, a passiflora, and one or two acacias: and this takes place so gradually, that the proprietors of such conservatories are often not aware of the result; just as in some pleasure-grounds a few strong shrubs are allowed to take the lead, and choke all the rest. We have generally found that the best kept conservatories are those where the master or mistress is without the cares of a family. A good beginning is made at first when the party is perhaps newly married, but with the increase of children there is a necessity for greater economy, and the conservatory is one of the first gardening scenes connected with the house that is neglected, or on which no expense for new plants and soil is bestowed. This is far from being the case at Garscube; but we make this and similar remarks as being the only means of giving any value to this notice, since, being at the time in bad health, and having taken no memorandums, we cannot pretend to give accurate descriptions.

The garden is cultivated in the Scotch manner, with flowers in the borders to the walks, and crops on the wall borders; two things ruinous to all expectations of abundant crops of fruit. Whenever we have represented this practice as no longer followed in the best gardens in England, and in many in Scotland, the question has been put to us, How shall we get our early crops of peas, potatoes, cauliflowers, &c.? The usual answer which we make to this question is that supplied by Mr. Errington, one of the most scientific and experienced practical gardeners in England, viz. that there is not an early crop of vegetables which could not be obtained within one week of those on a wall border, by making in the compartments artificial slopes to the south, and by careful protection.

We departed by another and most delightful approach through an irregular grove of oaks, elms, pines, firs, cedars, Portugal laurels, and hollies. This approach, as far as we can recollect, was on a comparatively level surface, constituting the top of a bank, which formed one of the boundaries of what doubtless was at one time a broad lake, with a river running

through it, but which is now low irregular ground with eminences which at one time had been islands. The place was moderately well kept, particularly the kitchen-garden, and though it rained the whole time that we were viewing it, we left it very much delighted.

GLASGOW. —Through the kindness of the Secretary of the Horticultural Society, we drove to the different public buildings and squares, and though we have nothing to say in the way of detail, we cannot help expressing our admiration of the many handsome street elevations, executed from the designs of Mr. Hamilton and his sons; and more particularly the new Banking House and the new Club House. We cannot leave Glasgow without mentioning the Eagle Inn, and its most obliging landlord, Mr. Fraser; for his accommodations and attention we found to be far beyond what are usually met with at such places. We were forcibly struck with the difference, when, about a month afterwards, we were obliged to pass through Glasgow, and stop at the Black Bull.

FROM GLASGOW TO UDDINGSTONE the road is broad, firm, and smooth, accompanied by an excellent footpath; the fences are in good repair, the hedges well trained, the stone walls substantial, and frequently of ashlar-work. The crops of wheat, potatoes, and oats, and clover and rye-grass, are most luxuriant, without the appearance of a single weed, except in the margins of the fences, where they are not unfrequent, and at present coming into flower. This is a crying sin throughout Scotland. With the finest crops in the interior of the field that could possibly be wished, the vilest weeds, such as docks and thistles, are found flowering and running to seed in the hedgerow margins. We cannot make an exception in favour of any part of the country between Stirling and Kinross on the north, and Berwick-upon-Tweed on the south.

We were particularly struck with the luxuriance of the weeds by the road sides in the neighbourhood of Paisley, and between that town and Glasgow; but we were soon able to account for it from the personal habits of the mass of the population, which are the very reverse of delicacy or cleanliness.

There ought certainly to be some general law, as there is in some parts of Belgium and Germany, that all weeds whatever ought to be cut down before they come into flower, and that when this is not done by the occupant of the land on which they grow, it ought to be effected by a district officer, whose business it should be to attend to this and other public nuisances, at the occupier's expense. In some parts of the Continent parochial rewards are given for the unexpanded flower-buds of weeds, for the cocoons of insects, and for the young of different sorts of vermin; but we are not yet arrived at this degree of agricultural nicety.

We cannot help remarking that in the midst of fields covered with the most luxuriant crops, the rows of cottages by the road side had the most miserable appearance. No variety in their form, magnitude, or materials; no difference in the size of their windows, or in their chimney tops; no porch; no front garden; no creepers or climbers on the walls; no flowers to be seen anywhere; and few or no windows, except those on the ground floor, to give the idea of a bed-room floor. The same line of dull stone side wall, and of slate, stone, or thatched roof; the walls with small windows, the broken panes of glass in which are often stuffed with rags; occur at intervals all along the road, forming a notable contrast with the wealth displayed in the villas, the farm-houses, the fields, and even the fences and roads.

TRENTHAM HALL – A VIEW IN THE GARDENS

TRENTHAM HALL – THE TERRACE

TRENTHAM HALL – THE PARTERRE

BOTHWELL CASTLE is known as one of the best kept large places in Scotland; and, what adds to the merit of the noble proprietor, he has no particular taste for gardening, and has the place equally well kept when he is absent as when he is resident. The ruins of the ancient castle and the modern house are both situated on the summit of a very high and steep bank, varied by old wood, which slopes precipitously to the Clyde; and the walks down to and along the river are numerous, and, as may be supposed, singularly grand and picturesque. We went over the whole of them in 1804 and 1806, but we could not, on this visit, undergo that fatigue. We were gratified to find, as far as we did go over them, that the style of keeping was exactly what, we recommend.

There was but a poor crop of fruit on the walls and espaliers which we attributed to the borders in both cases being cropped, and to the want of protection for the blossoms in spring.

Gentlemen in Scotland have no idea of the care and expense taken and incurred in England to protect the blossoms of wall fruit trees. If they have laid out a kitchen-garden and built the walls, they think it quite enough, just as a planter of forest trees thinks the work is finished when he has filled the ground with so many thousand plants per acre. By not cropping the borders, by thatching peach borders occasionally in rainy autumns to prevent the rain from penetrating them, thereby checking the growth and ripening the wood, and by careful covering with canvass during the blossoming season, crops of wall fruit might be rendered nearly as certain and as abundant as crops of gooseberries. But very few country gentlemen in Scotland would go to the necessary expense.

BOTHWELL CASTLE – 'THE RUINS OF THE ANCIENT CASTLE AND THE MODERN
HOUSE ARE BOTH SITUATED ON THE SUMMIT OF A VERY HIGH AND STEEP
BANK, VARIED BY OLD WOOD, WHICH SLOPES PRECIPITOUSLY TO THE CLYDE...'

JULY 28, 29. —The road from Bothwell Castle to the village of Hamilton presents some grand masses of wood on hilly ground, and crosses the Clyde and its steep rocky banks, also crowned with wood. The plantations belonging to the park of Hamilton Palace border the road on each side, from the bridge till we arrive at the village. This village, which in 1804, when we first saw it, was a dirty miserable place, with scarcely a good house except the inn, is now entirely changed. It contains a number of substantial houses, some in streets, but the greater number detached. The old inn is turned into the office of the Duke of Hamilton's land-steward, and there is a most substantial new inn built, in which we obtained most excellent fresh salmon and old whiskey, and the very best treatment; but very indifferent potatoes and other vegetables, from there being no market-gardener at Hamilton, and no early potatoes grown in the landlord's garden, and from every vegetable, except potatoes, being obtained from Glasgow. With respect to the greater part of the houses composing the village or town, as it may now be called, they are, we suppose, built on feus, which are generally leases of 999 years; and the builders, as almost everywhere else in Scotland, seem to have carefully avoided showing the least appearance of improved design or of ornament. But what forms the greatest objection to the detached houses of Hamilton is, that they have no front gardens, or, at least, we recollect very few, and they display no flowers or flowering shrubs.

HAMILTON PALACE is a noble pile of Roman architecture, standing in a park of 1700 acres. Through His Grace's kindness we were permitted to see the interior of the palace, which is admirably arranged, and superiorly finished and furnished. Among the ancient and curious furniture, are several cabinets, beds, chairs, tapestry, and other things, which belonged to Mary Queen of Scots; and many articles, also, which were once those of Marie Antoinette. Besides these, we saw such a profusion of articles, in china, glass, marble, silver, and gold, and of furniture ornamented with previous stones, as we should suppose is nowhere else to be found, either in Scotland or England, not even excepting Windsor Castle. The pictures are numerous, but we had only time to glance at them, and to notice "Daniel in the Lion's Den." The proportions of all the modern rooms are satisfactory, the chimney-pieces superb, and the carving of the mahogany doors and other fittings most elaborate. One of the most striking and imposing rooms, which is called the Tribune, is a lofty saloon, lighted from the ceiling, with rich projecting galleries, and forming a centre of communication to a suite of state-rooms. The hall and grand staircase were being finished with black marble, of which we saw numerous columns, but we had only an imperfect glance at them from the scaffolding. The exterior of the building is grand and imposing, from its magnitude, and the unity of architectural design which pervades every part of all the elevations; and the same character of grandeur being preserved within, and heightened by richness of finishing and furniture, becomes magnificence.

Nothing has been done to the grounds around the house, or at least nothing at all worthy of such a building. There are various systems on which the grounds of such a palace might be laid out. Supposing the ancient system were to be adopted, then the first step would be to form the main public roads leading to and from the palace into straight avenues for as many miles as they pass through the property, the palace forming the central object. Next we would turn the Clyde in such a manner as that the avenues should cross it on suitable bridges

HAMILTON PALACE – 'A NOBLE PILE OF ROMAN ARCHITECTURE, STANDING IN A
PARK OF 1700 ACRES.'

at right angles, immediately before arriving at the gates. The public roads would at a distance, to strangers driving along them, appear to terminate in magnificent gates leading to the palace; but the roads would, on arriving there, be turned so as to pass outside the park.

The expense would, no doubt, be great; but we are not considering the expense, but only what would be suitable for the grounds of such palace, if they had been laid out in the days of Louis XIV. The house we would surround on three sides with an extensive architectural flower-garden, including a large architectural conservatory, in the form of a Grecian temple, attached to the mansion by an arcade or colonnade.

CADZOW CASTLE – 'IN THIS PARK THERE IS A HERD OF WILD SCOTTISH CATTLE,
IN WHICH THE PREVAILING COLOUR IS WHITE. THEY ARE SAID TO BE MUCH LESS
FEROCIOUS THAN THE WILD CATTLE OF CHILLINGHAM.'

CADZOW CASTLE, the ancient baronial residence of the family of Hamilton, is situated on the top of a steep bank of the river Evan, which joins the Clyde near one of the entrances to Hamilton Palace. The old castle is approached through the remains of a forest of oaks, having from their age mostly the character of old decaying pollards

In this park there is a herd of wild Scottish cattle, in which the prevailing colour is white. They are said to be much less ferocious than the wild cattle of Chillingham.

We went to the old ornamental building called Chatelherault, and found it occupied

CHATELHERAULT – '...OCCUPIED BY A SOLITARY GARDENER.'

by a solitary gardener, who, nevertheless, contrives to entertain himself in the evenings with the gardening newspapers, *Chamber's Journal,* and other periodicals.

JULY 29. —HAMILTON TO ALLANTON. Leaving the valley of the Clyde, we pass over a tract of land, which, forty years ago, was little better than a moor, but which is now varied by hedge-rows and plantations, and traversed by good roads. The walls of the labourers' cottages are generally of stone; yet, with all this care of outward appearance in the building, these cottages have scarcely ever a front garden, or any flowers or flowering shrubs between them and the road. They have, however, generally placed over the entrance door, a stone, with the initials of the husband and wife, and the year in which the cottage was built by them, which it is always satisfactory to see.

MILTON LOCKHART, THE SEAT OF [-] LOCKHART, ESQ., M.P., brother to the celebrated editor of the *Quarterly Review,* is a very old place, celebrated in *Old Mortality* as the residence of Claverhouse. A new house, by Burns, in his peculiar combination of the old Scotch, or Belgian, style and the Tudor Gothic, is just finished. It stands on a prominent point of a peninsula formed by a remarkable turn of the Clyde; which, after washing the base of the bank on which the house stands, darts away from it across the valley, and, after a course of, we should suppose, above a mile, returns to another bank near the house, enclosing, as it were in a loop, a beautiful piece of meadow scenery, fringed with trees on the banks of the river.

At present, nothing is finished but the house; and all the ground work is at a stand-still, and likely to be so for some time, on account of electioneering expenses. We went over every part of the house, from the cellars to the garrets, and found in it, everything which a villa, or rather a mansion, ought to contain, though on a small scale. When Milton Lockhart is finished, it will be a residence of great beauty and variety, from the contrast of the

215

MILTON LOCKHART HOUSE – 'A NEW HOUSE, BY BURNS…IS JUST FINISHED.'

architectural gardens at the house, with the romantic windings and picturesque banks of the river, and the wooded hilly scenery which extends on every side.

In the flower-garden we found a collection of sweet-williams which surpassed in beauty every thing of the kind that we had before seen. The gardener had been collecting them for several years.

MILTON LOCKHART TO LANARK. The ride from Hamilton to Lanark, along the banks of the Clyde, has long been celebrated for its beauty, and it forms a very good study for the landscape-gardener who has walks to form along the banks of a natural river. Here he may see the effect of such bends in the walk as command long reaches of the river, and others which merely look across it; of seeing the water from an open glade, and from a dark thicket; of seeing it near at hand, and at a distance; of the walk being parallel to the river's course, of going away from it, and approaching it; and, in particular, he will learn the fine effect of some of these changes, when accompanied by the sound of a waterfall, now rising and now dying away on the ear. The inn at Lanark is a larger house than that at Hamilton, but in point of comfort it is far inferior.

JULY 30.—CARTLAND CRAGS, a remarkable chasm with rocky sides, overhung with trees, and rich in wild plants, and also the Stonebyre Falls of the Clyde, afforded us much enjoyment, but we cannot stop to describe them.

JULY 30. TO AUGUST 1. — COREHOUSE; LORD COREHOUSE. This is decidedly the grandest place on the banks of the Clyde, embracing, as it does, a very extensive reach of the river, including the celebrated Falls of the Clyde, and the Bonnington Falls.

The entrance lodge to Corehouse is close to the Bridge of Lanark; and the approach

216

COREHOUSE – 'THIS IS DECIDEDLY THE GRANDEST PLACE ON THE BANKS OF THE CLYDE.'

road is upwards of a mile in length, along the banks of the river, but so much above it as only at intervals to show the water. The line of road, which, in respect to its surface, is always nearly level, in regard to its direction is beautifully varied by natural and artificial woody scenery, by views extending into the interior to where the distant hills belonging to the estate are crowned with thriving plantations, and by views across the river to the village of New Lanark. Here are the extensive cotton-mills where the celebrated Robert Owen first tried his philanthropic experiments. We scarcely know any thing finer, in the way of appropriated scenery, than the effect of the plantations about New Lanark, and thence to Bonnington, as seen from the approach to Corehouse, and the grounds about the house; and the appearance of the grounds and woods of Corehouse is doubtless equally effective, as seen from the opposite side of the river.

The house is in the old English domestic manner of Mr. Blore; simple, grand, and with an elevated terrace on three sides. The interior contains apartments, large, lofty, and well-arranged, opening into a spacious hall. There is none of that confused appearance sometimes found in modern Gothic houses, which are often crowded with turrets, bell-towers, and chimney-tops, without; and traversed by narrow passages, and over-done with Gothic cornices and other Gothic ornaments, within.

All the natural woods at Corehouse abound in wild herbaceous plants; and in early spring the primrose, and afterwards the wild hyacinth, the stellaria, and the foxglove, form fine masses of colour: but the effect of the numerous wild plants here has been increased, to a degree which the botanist alone can value, by planting and sowing among them many kinds of perennials and annuals, including the hardier bulbs.

We cannot pretend to describe any part of Corehouse in detail, though, from the kind hospitality of the proprietor, we had an opportunity of looking over the grounds for two days; but the extent of the walks and the variety of the scenery are so great, that to do so would require either a longer period, or the assistance of notes and sketches to refresh the memory. We left Corehouse; and the kind and most intelligent family of Lord Corehouse, with deep regret, and can only console ourselves by hoping that, at some future time, we may have an opportunity of visiting both again.

We were sorry to observe, by a Railroad Report then just issued from parliament, that a line of road is projected to pass through the estate of Corehouse, between the house and the stable offices. Fortunately there is little chance of this line being carried into execution, otherwise it would completely destroy Corehouse as a country residence.

AUGUST 2.—PEEBLES TO MELROSE. The country is beautifully varied by hills, some of which are wooded, and others cultivated, and exhibiting fields of turnips, and barley or wheat, to the very summits.

TRAQUAIR. We went through that curious old place, Traquair, where the kitchen-garden walls are 18ft. high, and were coped with turf now bearing a rich crop of grass and weeds, the seeds of which were nearly ready for being distributed over the garden by the winds. In this garden were excellent crops, particularly of strawberries, but we did not find the gardener at home. In the herb ground we found elecampane, lovage, horehound, and a number of other herbs formerly cultivated in all gardens, but now generally neglected. Traquair House has nothing modern about it, not even a full-sized sash window, and the main entrance has no gravelled road up to it; as, till lately, was the case at Knowle in Kent, and, by imitation of old

TRAQUAIR – 'ALTOGETHER IT IS A GREAT CURIOSITY AS A GENTLEMAN'S
RESIDENCE.'

BOTHWELL CASTLE

MELROSE ABBEY

places, at Fonthill Abbey. There is a grand terrace on the other front, and the main body of the house is flanked by square pavilions. Altogether it is a great curiosity as a gentleman's residence; and it was not without difficulty that we obtained liberty to drive up to it, the Earl of Traquair being from home. We arrived at Melrose in time to see the ruins of the abbey with good daylight, and we remained among them till it was dark.

AUGUST 3.—MELROSE TO DALKEITH, BY DRYBURGH ABBEY AND THIRLSTANE CASTLE. The ruins of Melrose Abbey are, perhaps, the best preserved ruins of the kind in Scotland, though they admit of the improvement of showing the whole of the original floor, by removing from it the heaps of rubbish with which it is now disfigured. The accompanying burying-ground is extensive and not over-crowded with graves, and it might be surrounded and intersected with some straight gravel walks; and along these might be planted a few Irish yews, and other evergreens, chiefly of cypress-like shapes, which would afford agreeable walks for the inhabitants, and display the abbey to advantage to strangers.

DRYBURGH ABBEY; THE EARL OF BUCHAN. Great pains were taken with this place by a former earl, who planted an extensive orchard, many cedars of Lebanon, and other ornamental trees, and erected some ornamental buildings. We regret to say that the whole place appeared to us in a state of neglect, and no part more so than the grounds about the ruins. The sheep were injuring the fruit trees and the cedars, by rubbing against their stems, and the cattle breaking down the fences. The ruins are extensive, but they are too much encumbered with trees and shrubs, and, what is worse, with dug ground and flowers. Dug ground about an old building, when carried to any extent, always gives the idea of yesterday, and checks the feeling of veneration which would otherwise predominate. The floors of the interior of these ruins are heaped up with rubbish, and overgrown with rank plants, and there is a damp vault set round with busts of stucco, such as are sold in the streets, which are shown by the guide, who evidently thinks them of far more importance, and more deserving of attention, than the ruins themselves. The poor woman who shows these busts and gives them names knows no better; but what are we to think of the proprietor of the place, who permits such things? By nature Dryburgh Abbey has immense advantages, and these ruins are objects of intense interest, which might be turned to good account in rendering the place worthy of respect and admiration, instead of creating, as it now does, feelings of an opposite nature.

THIRLSTANE CASTLE; THE EARL OF LAUDER. After passing a number of gentlemen's seats possessing many natural beauties, but exhibiting very little good architecture or landscape-gardening, the absence of the latter easily ascertained by the isolated clumps and the want of scattered trees in the parks and lawns, we come to Lauder, close to which is Thirlstane Castle. The building is of great antiquity, and, besides one or two very ancient rooms, it contains a number which were richly finished in the Louis XIV. style, prevalent in the time of Charles II. These rooms are chiefly remarkable for their gorgeous ceilings, exhibiting wreaths of fruit, foliage, and flowers, in very high relief; arabesques of extraordinary combinations; and, in some of the rooms, domes raised in the centres of the ceilings, and painted in imitation of the sky, with gilt stars. The beauties of arabesque decoration are not generally understood. Many object to them because they are not natural, but it is their fanciful character which constitutes their beauty. Reason gives up the reins to the fancy, and we delight to be led about by that power into regions where every thing is not only new but

THIRLSTANE CASTLE – 'THE BUILDING IS OF GREAT ANTIQUITY.'

strange. Nonsense in the midst of sense is often a relief to a mind kept on the rack, and arabesques are the nonsense of high art. Thirlstane Castle is undergoing extensive alterations and additions under the direction of Mr. Burns, and, when finished, will probably be one of the finest things of the kind in Scotland.

The landlord of the inn at Lauder has travelled a good deal in America, and is very intelligent. It is always refreshing to meet with a man who has seen the world, but more especially when this is unexpected.

In descending from the Lammermuir hills, we look down on the rich plain of the Lothians as on a map. Pass on the left some overpruned plantations of larches, and on the right a temperance hotel. An excellent inn at Dalkeith.

The road from Dalkeith to Edinburgh is broad, kept in excellent repair, and passes through a country so much altered from what it was in 1806, when we last saw it, that we should never have recognised it to be the same territory. Every farmyard has now a high, and often handsome, chimney for its steam-engine, which reminds us much more of Birmingham than of any part of Scotland, except Glasgow. The low round towers, often with the walls ragged at top, so as to give the idea of the remains of the high towers, built over the orifices of the old coal pits, are also to us a new feature; to which we must add, that the direction of the road has been changed, in some places so much so that we could not recognise Libberton Kirk (where we went to school in 1796), and that plantations newly made when we left the country are now grown up, furnishing by their thinnings useful timber. We were much gratified with the prevalence of the balsam poplar in the plantations at St. Catherine's near Edinburgh, because that is the first tree that comes into leaf in the spring in every part of the northern hemisphere, and nothing can be more beautiful than the delicate gamboge yellow of its foliage when it first expands.

We stopped at present only one night in Edinburgh, and, after dining at an advertising hotel in Princes Street, and being imposed on both by the master and servants, we took an incognito stroll in the old town, and visited some of the closes and wynds that were formerly familiar to us. Nothing struck us more forcibly than the appearance of the Norloch, covered with trees that were not even planted when we left Edinburgh.

AUGUST 6. —EDINBURGH TO KINROSS. At North Queen's Ferry we went to see a beautifully situated small place which once belonged to Captain Maconnochie, author of *Australiana,* now in Australia, and where his amiable and accomplished lady displayed her taste and skill in the flower-garden. The outer gate was open, and we passed through the whole place, including the lawn, shrubbery, and kitchen-garden, without seeing a human being.

CULROSS ABBEY was the ancient seat of the Dundonald family, and the building, though in ruins, was held in much veneration by the country round, till it was almost entirely pulled down by the late Sir Robert Preston, who, however, made the *amende* by building the present abbey in an ancient style. The place is chiefly remarkable for a lime tree avenue, and a terrace walk bordered by a high wall of pear trees, and terminated by alcove seats.

AUGUST 10. — STIRLING. We devoted this day to seeing the castle, Messrs. Drummond's Agricultural Museum, the King's Knot, supposed to be the gardens of James II., the Bowling Green, and some other places. There are many curious architectural remains in the castle, which, owing to some misunderstanding between the governor and the keeper, we

STIRLING CASTLE – 'THERE ARE MANY CURIOUS ARCHITECTURAL REMAINS IN THE CASTLE, WHICH, OWING TO SOME MISUNDERSTANDING BETWEEN THE GOVERNOR AND THE KEEPER, WE HAD GREAT DIFFICULTY IN SEEING.'

had great difficulty in seeing. There never appears to have been any good taste in the architecture; for the proportions of the members are clumsy, and the sculpture and statuary incorrect and unpoetical imitations. The view of the Forth from the castle is reckoned one of the finest things of the kind in the world; but at the time we saw it it was low water, and we could not detect the windings of the river.

MESSRS. DRUMMOND'S AGRICULTURAL MUSEUM is the first concern of the kind that was established in Scotland, and it is impossible too highly to estimate the good which it has done, not only in the immediate neighbourhood, but throughout Scotland; we might even say throughout the world, for Messrs. Drummond not only send agricultural implements to England and Ireland, but to the East and West Indies, and to North and South America.

The most remarkable garden antiquity about Stirling, or indeed in Scotland, is a piece of ground which, at some former period, has been laid out in terraces and slopes, and probably surrounded by a canal. Messrs. Drummond furnished the following extracts: —

NOTICES OF THE KING'S KNOT AT STIRLING CASTLE. —In the gardens is a mound of earth in form of a table, called the Knot, with benches of earth around, where, according to tradition, the court sometimes had *fetes champetre*. Vestiges of the walks and parterres, with a few stumps of trees, are still visible.

THE KING'S GARDENS. —Their present condition is that of a marshy piece of pasture ground completely desolated, so far as shrubs and flowers are concerned. The utmost exertion of the memory of the present generation can only recollect an old cherry tree which stood at the corner of one of the parterres, and which was burnt down by the wadding of a shot which some thoughtless sportsman fired into its decayed trunk, as he happened to pass it on his way home from the fields. An octagonal mount in the centre of the supposed garden is called "The King's Knote," and is said by tradition to have been the scene of some forgotten play or recreation, which the king used to enjoy on that spot with his court. In an earlier age this strange object seems to have been called "The Round Table," and, in all probability, it was the scene of the out-of-doors game of that name, founded upon the history of King Arthur, and of which the courtly personages of former times are known to have been fond.

224

8

TRAVELS IN

Devon, Cornwall and Somerset

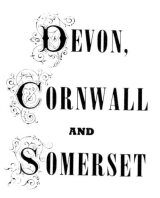

SEPTEMBER 1842

AUGUST 29. —LONDON TO NETTLECOMBE COURT, THE SEAT OF SIR JOHN TREVELYAN, BART. The greater part of the country, as seen from the rail-road, is rich and varied; and from Paddington to Maidenhead it is in many places delightful.

At Hanwell, where the rail-road is on a high embankment, we look down upon a parsonage surrounded by grass fields, and with gardens and shrubberies, all the walks and other details of which were so distinct, with their lights and shadows that we could not help comparing them to a map. There is a degree of satisfaction in tracing the resemblance of nature to art, as well as there is in tracing that of art to nature. The country roads seen here and in other places crossing under the embankments of the rail-road seem, in a great measure, to have lost their use and importance; and they remind us that the progress of all improvement involves the deterioration or ruin of something of the same kind that had gone before.

Near Reading, Caversham House, has a magnificent appearance; having been greatly enlarged by the present proprietor, Mr. Crashaw. The scenery beyond Reading includes occasional glimpses of the Thames, and is remarkably umbrageous and rich, exhibiting some fine trees.

On both sides of the Swindon station, the country is flat and apparently uninteresting; but the station itself is the handsomest we have yet seen. At this station, which is considered half-way between London and Taunton, there are four large refreshment rooms, two on each side of the road, of noble proportions, and finished in the most exquisite style; with the walls paneled, Sylvester's fireplaces, and beautifully painted ceilings. Such rooms cannot fail greatly to improve the taste of every one who enters them; and, in this respect alone, the proprietors of the rail-road are entitled to the best thanks of the country. The rail-road buildings on this, and indeed on every line, afford fine examples of beauty arising from no other consideration than that of fitness for the end in view.

We arrived at *Bridgewater* at 2 o'clock, and found a Minehead coach waiting for passengers, by which we proceeded to Williton, where we arrived at 5 o'clock. The road is hilly, but we passed through some curious old villages, and observed several villas, one or two of which still retain clipped yew hedges, and other vestiges of the geometric style.

The road, nevertheless, is conducted without either skill or taste, though it might be led on one uniform slope down the declivities and across the combes (valleys), so as to render it easy either for ascent or descent. We arrived at Nettlecombe Court at 6 o'clock.

AUGUST 29. TO SEPTEMBER 5. — NETTLECOMBE COURT. The road to this place from Williton is up the bottom of a winding combe, or valley, consisting of water meadows, woods, white cottages and their gardens, and some quarries, a fine brook, and hedge-row trees. Here is a water-mill, supplied with water by means of a course the sides and bottom of which are of stone laid in the Aberthaw lime, which has the property of setting under water, and being in that and other respects equal to Roman cement. The rock which produces this lime extends across from Wales, and proves of immense value both to builders and farmers. We passed a cottage, the walls of which were covered with the broad and narrow-leaved myrtle, both 12ft. high, and overspread with bloom; large hydrangeas, which become blue naturally in most places that we have seen them in both Somersetshire and Devonshire; and near Nettlecombe church some immense elms. We had not an opportunity of looking at the

grounds of Nettlecombe Court till the following morning, when we were astonished and delighted with the view from the windows of the house, looking up the steep sides of the rounded hills that rose on every side, and which were mostly crowned with old oak woods. The immense difference between this kind of scenery, and any thing that is to be met with within a 100 miles of London, produced the effect alluded to; and we found it to be a sort of key-note to the impressions made by the scenery of Somersetshire and Devonshire generally. Rounded hills covered with grass to the top, with winding valleys having sloping sides; the valleys more or less wide, and the sides of hills differing in degrees of steepness; occasionally with water in the bottom in the form of a small stream or brook, and rarely of a river or an inlet of the sea, characterise the greater part of the scenery of Somersetshire, and at least of the South of Devonshire. There is not even a sharply pointed hill, or one with concave sides; and certainly nothing that can be compared to hills similarly covered with grass in the South of Scotland. In England, however, the rich wooded valleys have no parallel in Scotland; and Somersetshire and Devonshire only require to have some features of the agriculture of Scotland and Northern England joined to their excellent grass-land husbandry, to exemplify the highest degree of cultivation of which such a country is susceptible.

Before we proceed farther, we must notice one or two characteristics of Somersetshire and Devonshire. The first is, that the soil is almost every where red, deep, and fertile; the second, that, the surface being generally under grass, there is a predominance of green in the landscape; and the third, which, we suppose, is the consequence of the other two, is, that the cottages, villas, and dwellings, of every description, are white-washed. The desire for this white appearance we suppose to be a physical result of the prevalence of green and red; white, though it cannot be called a complementary colour to these, as green is to red, being yet a relief to the eye, on similar principles.

The high banks on which the hedges are planted form the next characteristic of these

227

counties, rendering it difficult to see the adjoining fields or country from the road, and being really a great nuisance to a stranger. We have also to complain of the narrowness and depth of the lanes, or parish roads, and the general want of guide-posts. Another characteristic is the form of the churches, which have very high square towers, each with a small round tower attached, containing a staircase; the square towers sometimes, though rarely, terminating in spires, as at the little dirty Scotch-looking village called Marlborough, and the ancient town of Modbury, both between Salcombe and Plymouth.

Nettlecombe Court is a seat of great extent; and, though we took an extensive drive every day while we remained there, we did not see all the farms. The drives are exceedingly varied and beautiful, and exhibit fine combinations of pasture and woodland, comfortable cottages, and most substantial farm-houses and farmeries.

There is an admirable kitchen-garden here, with the walls covered with the very best kinds of peaches, nectarines, and pears, all in fine order, while the fig ripens as a standard. We observed a very excellent kind of cabbage, which we were informed, by the gardener, Mr. Elworthy, was raised between the Paington and Cornish cabbages, and which is called the Nettlecombe cabbage. In the pleasure-ground there is an old stone quarry, the bottom of which has been levelled, and the side planted with half-hardy plants, including several plants of *Capparis spinosa*; which will, doubtless, at some future time, supply the family with capers, as the lemon trees on the garden walls in this part of the country do with lemons.

The great novelty and charm of Nettlecombe are, that, the house being situated in a bottom, the scenery on every side is looked up to, instead of being looked over; the effect of which, united with the immense masses of wood, is romantic in a very high degree. Some of the valleys are so deep, that the sun does not shine into them, for between two and three months every winter.

In consequence of the bold undulations and deep valleys, the shadows produced by the varying position of the sun are continually changing; increasing in one place and diminishing in another, so as to form a perpetual variety, greatly heightened by the groups formed by the deer.

The church and churchyard at Nettlecombe are close to the house. The former is kept in excellent repair; as are the family monuments, some of which existed as far back as the time of the crusades. Having a great respect for the antiquity of families, a long descent of ancestry being one of the few things which no human exertions, no wealth, and not even chance can procure, we were much gratified by a sight of the Trevelyan family papers, from the time of Edward I.; almost all of which were in excellent preservation. Among the oldest of these were many permissions from the church to eat meat during Lent; and one pardon from Henry VIII. to a Trevelyan for killing a man in chance-medley. Tradition, however, traces back the family much higher than the written records; as it is said that the head of a

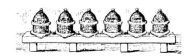

CEDRUS DEODARA AT BICTON

ABIES DOUGLASII AT BICTON

swimming horse, in the family arms, relates to a Trevelyan who was on one of the Scilly Islands when it sank in 850, and that he saved himself by swimming on shore on horseback.

FATTENING SWINE WITH FERN, OR BRAKE (Pteris aquilina). Among the many curious and useful things which Mr. Babbage related to us was the following, which we give in his own words.

"Walking over the estate one day in the spring, I saw a man and his family busily employed gathering the young shoots of fern. On enquiry I found it was to feed their pig. Having expressed a doubt as to its nutritious quality, the man said it was equal to potatoes, and that he would undertake to feed a pig with it alone, and at the end of a month produce the pig in as good condition as another pig that had been fed with potatoes. The way to prepare the fern is to boil (or rather simmer) it for two hours in an iron pot: when cold, it forms a strong jelly."

DUNSTER CASTLE; [-] LUTTRELL, ESQ. This is a fine old castle, situated high up the side of a conical hill on the sea coast; with a park, consisting of a valley opening to the sea, with the sides finely clothed with wood. The meadows are mown or pastured, and appear as smooth as a lawn; while those parts of the hill sides not covered with wood exhibit ferns, hollies, and thorns, unmixed with foreign trees, and in such a state as we may suppose they were in when the castle was built, in the time of Henry VIII. or Elizabeth. There is no want of scenery of this kind in the parks of England, but it is not often that it belongs to a really old castle, with all its grandeur and simplicity. Many modern castles have, in our opinion, so much architectural display exteriorly, that we never for a moment suppose them to be old. The ancient entrance to Dunster Castle is through the straight street of Dunster town, the gateway to the Castle forming its termination. The actual entrance, at present, is by a winding road, which gradually ascends the hill to the Castle court. The Castle is surrounded by terraces; and against the walls are some fine exotics, among which are a large lemon tree protected by glass during winter, a large pomegranate, large myrtles, passion flowers, wistarias, coronillas, and an immense hydrangea with both blue and pink flowers as a finale. Higher up than the Castle court, on the summit of the hill, is an oval bowling green, approached by a winding path, which commands a panoramic view of the surrounding country, including the bold promontory of Minehead, the sea, and the mountains of South Wales. The whole place was in excellent order.

DUNSTER CASTLE – 'THIS IS A FINE OLD CASTLE, SITUATED HIGH UP THE SIDE OF
A CONICAL HILL ON THE SEA COAST.'

SEPTEMBER 5. — NETTLECOMBE TO EXETER, THROUGH TIVERTON. The road as far as Bampton was extremely hilly, consisting of narrow lanes, with their fences so high that the eye was either carried over the adjoining fields to such hilly ground as was near at hand, or, where hills were wanting, there was nothing seen but the steep high banks of the farms which bordered the deep and ditch-like road. At Bampton, the cottages have their chimney-tops finished with slates, sometimes two forming a triangle, and sometimes one large slate supported by four props, and kept from being blown away by a stone, as in the lake scenery.

From Tiverton to Exeter the road follows the course of the Exe, which passes through a finely wooded valley; and, were it not for the high road-side fences, it would be exquisitely beautiful. It is impossible, however, to enjoy this or any other scenery properly from the public roads, on account of the height of the fences.

The church at Tiverton contains some curious carving, particularly in a chapel erected long after the church; on the exterior of which was represented an extensive sea-scene with ships, proving, as all such scenes do, that the artist did not know the proper province of sculpture, which is to represent single objects, or foreground groups, and never subjects requiring the effect of distance.

POWDERHAM CASTLE, THE EARL OF DEVON. The fine magnolia trees and other exotics here are sadly neglected; the branches are unpruned, the stems covered with lichens and moss, and the plants choked up in many places with the commonest trees and shrubs. The house is being altered by Mr. Fowler, a guarantee to our minds that the general effect will be simple and grand. Some walled-up banks along the approach appeared to us much too common-place for the vicinity of a castle. Had there been rocks to penetrate, as at Warwick Castle, the case would have been different; but here the walling mode seems to have been adopted as a matter of choice, or for the sake of economy. We would have brought down the ground with a gentle slope, and had 3 or 4 feet of perfectly level surface on each side of the road.

POWDERHAM CASTLE – 'THE FINE MAGNOLIA TREES AND OTHER EXOTICS HERE ARE SADLY NEGLECTED; THE BRANCHES ARE UNPRUNED, THE STEMS COVERED WITH LICHENS AND MOSS AND THE PLANTS CHOKED UP IN MANY PLACES WITH THE COMMONEST TREES AND SHRUBS.'

SEPTEMBER 8. — FROM EXETER, BY LUSCOMBE, DAWLISH, TEIGNMOUTH, AND BABBICOMBE, TO TORQUAY. We set out in an open carriage with elevated seats, so as to see over the high fences, which every where border the roads and lanes. The day, like almost every other while we were in Devonshire, was fine; and the country and the sea rich, varied, and altogether delightful; all the corn carried; the turnip fields covered with luxuriant leaves; the rank pastures well stocked with red oxen and sheep; and the apple trees, which accompany every house and cottage, laden with fruit. We passed through Kenton, and other villages or groups of cottages, and saw some churches with high square towers, venerable and grand; and many cottages with cob walls, and thatched roofs. Rather too many of these and of larger dwellings had the walls whitewashed; which, though good in a moral point of view, as conveying the idea of care and cleanliness, is yet bad with reference to picturesque effect; because white spots do not harmonise with the surrounding colours, but remain for ever the same glaring objects, except during twilight and night. "In any scene where harmony prevails" says Sir Uvedale Price, "the least discordance in colour disturbs the eye, but if we suppose a single object of a glaring white to be introduced, the whole attention, in spite of all our efforts to the contrary will be drawn to that one point; a whitened object is already lighted up; it remains so when every thing else has retired into obscurity; it still forces itself into notice, still impudently stares you in the face. An object of a sober tint, unexpectedly gilded by the sun, is like a serious countenance suddenly lighted up by a smile; a whitened object like the eternal grin of a fool."

The views of the sea, and of the scenery all along the coast, are varied and beautiful; though the houses at Teignmouth and other watering places convey more the idea of the temporary residences of visitors and invalids, than of permanent abodes.

LUSCOMBE CASTLE – 'WELL KNOWN FOR ITS BEAUTY AND THE HIGH ORDER IN
WHICH EVERY THING EVEN TO THE FARM OFFICES, IS KEPT.'

LUSCOMBE CASTLE; CHARLES HOARE, ESQ. Well known for its beauty and the high order in which every thing, even to the farm offices, is kept. The grounds are said to have been originally laid out by the late Mr. John Veitch, father of the present nurseryman of that name. The castle is placed on the side of an ascending valley, and the two sides of this narrow valley are beautifully varied by trees, which thicken into woods as they approach the summits of the two ridges, so that the house may be said to stand on the side of a valley surrounded by hanging woods. There are a number of large magnolias and other choice trees and shrubs. Among the trees of which we took notes were: in the kitchen-garden, an olive 12ft. high and 8ft. wide, after being twelve years planted; another, 13ft. high and 10ft. wide; both these plants have ripened fruit; Callistemon salignus, 12ft. high and 6ft. wide, lemons, citrons, and limes, 12ft. high.

We found *Scilla verna* in flower as well as in seed on the downs, owing to the great heat of the summer and the recent rains; a circumstance which, we were afterwards informed by Mr. Gullet, the gardener at Woodbine Cottage, was not unusual.

TORQUAY. A delightful little sea-port and bathing-place, with cottages, villas, and lodging-houses, from the sea-shore to the summits of the rocky wooded hills with which the bay is surrounded. Some of these are in good taste, and almost all of them exhibit marks of care and design, both in the house and grounds, which, being evidence of progress, is sure to lead to good taste in the end. The grounds in several instances have been laid out and planted under the direction of Mr. Gullet.

WOODBINE COTTAGE; MISS JOHNES. The whole is kept in excellent order by Mr. Gullet, who is unquestionably, not only an excellent gardener, but a man of genius as a sculptor and mechanic. To be convinced of this, it is only necessary to see the numerous figures which he has cut out in wood with his knife during the winter evenings, some of which are portraits of well known characters at Torquay; and the manner in which he has brought water from a distant hill, across a valley, and over an intervening hill, by a siphon.

Miss Johnes, the proprietress of Torquay, is sister to the late Colonel Johnes of Hafod in Cardiganshire, a splendid place, where we had the pleasure of passing a few days professionally, so long ago as 1805. Miss Johnes is upwards of ninety years of age, and in perfect health.

BERRY POMEROY CASTLE; THE DUKE OF SOMERSET. This is the ruins of what has been a lofty and widely extending castle; but it is now shorn of much of its dignity, by the duke's tenantry having, till within the last twenty years, taken away almost all the master stones of the building, such as the lintels and jambs to the doors, windows, and fireplaces. To prevent the walls of the castle from literally tumbling down, the place of these lintels was supplied some years ago by oak beams, and that of the jambs by common rubble stonework. This gives the whole ruin a mean appearance, and destroys the idea of great age; for no building with wooden lintels can last for centuries. Another circumstance which greatly detracts from its dignity is its being overwhelmed with trees. Such, however, is the height of the walls, and of the well defined portions which occur here and there, for example the gatehouse, that, were it not for the want of the master stones, it would not be difficult to render this a grand and impressive ruin; and to restore in it one or two rooms, so as to form a habitation for a person to take care of the whole. The views from the castle must, from its elevation, be very

BERRY POMEROY CASTLE – 'ANOTHER CIRCUMSTANCE WHICH GREATLY
DETRACTS FROM ITS DIGNITY IS ITS BEING OVERWHELMED WITH TREES.'

extensive; but it is so shrouded in trees, that we can only see over the precipitous terrace walls to a deep valley, the sides and bottom of which are covered with ancient wood.

Sharpham; [-] Durant, Esq. The road from Totness to Sharpham is a crooked narrow lane between high banks, in which two carriages can with difficulty pass. If widened and carried along an improved line, which might be almost on a perfect level, it would be one of the loveliest drives in the world, from the abundance of wood and the great beauty of the valley of the Dart, the water of which expands so as to resemble a winding lake. The narrow lane alluded to is two or three miles in length; and the approach road, after leaving the lodge, extends upwards of a mile. The house is very well placed on a projecting platform, which forms, as it were, the corner between the valley of the Dart and another valley, which may be called that of Sharpham. Here the "sufficient reason" for choosing the situation is obvious at a glance. There is much natural beauty at this place, and many fine woods and trees; but it is in a state of sad neglect, nothing having been done to it for several years. It appears, indeed, never to have been completed; for the walls of the kitchen-garden have not been built, and there are the rafters of a vinery, under which vines are trained, but for which, we were informed, the sashes were never made. The feeling of melancholy which such a place as this produces is so mixed up with misery, that it affords no pleasure; whereas, an old neglected place, where there is no evidence of the the neglect being the result of want of means, fills the mind with a feeling of veneration and respect, as well as sadness. A young or new place in a state of neglect or disorder affords an example of melancholy and misery; while an old full-grown place, uninhabited, in which nothing seems to be doing but keeping the place in tolerable order, is an example of melancholy and grandeur. To remove the idea of hopeless melancholy from an old place, there ought to be signs of life and improvement, if it were nothing more than the planting here and there of young trees where the old ones have been cut down. An old place, with nothing but old trees, leaves the mind without hope. There is

BERRY POMEROY CASTLE – 'NOW SHORN OF MUCH OF ITS DIGNITY BY THE
DUKE'S TENANTRY HAVING, TILL WITHIN THE LAST TWENTY YEARS, TAKEN
AWAY NEARLY ALL THE MASTER STONES OF THE BUILDING.'

239

nothing to look forward to but their decay; but an old place, with both old and young trees, more especially if it has been long in possession of the same family, and that family have children, is, we think, better calculated to give a feeling of perpetual existence to the proprietor for the time being, than any other state of things that we can conceive, unless it be that of a hereditary sovereign. One of the finest things at Sharpham is a broad walk from the house, along the side of a steep valley, to the head of that valley, where it crosses over by the gardener's cottage to a similar walk on the opposite side; the walk all the while winding much in direction, but being always nearly on a level. We were informed that it is continued through the woods towards the sea, exhibiting many fine views of the Dart and its opposite banks.

SEPTEMBER 9. — KINGSBRIDGE TO COMBE ROYAL, AND BY THE MOULT, WOODVILLE, SALCOMBE, AND MARLBOROUGH, TO MODBURY. In the garden of the inn at Kingsbridge is a

FLEET HOUSE – 'THE HOUSE IS OF CONSIDERABLE ANTIQUITY AND WELL PLACED.'

large lemon tree, protected by glass during winter, but without fire-heat, which supplies lemons enough for the use of the inn. The horse-keeper is the gardener, and being fond of that business, has the garden in excellent order. A few books are to be found in the inn, but nothing to what there ought to be; no county histories or local topography.

SEPTEMBER 10. — MODBURY TO FLEET HOUSE, KITLEY, SALTRAM, AND PLYMOUTH. Modbury is an ancient town of considerable size, without either a good inn or a bookseller's shop. We were informed that there was a subscription library for the better class; but we did not see the slightest evidence of intelligence or intellectual enjoyment among the mass.

FLEET HOUSE; J. BULTEEL, ESQ. The house is of considerable antiquity and well placed, and it is undergoing great improvement under the immediate direction of the proprietor, who is his own architect, and is, perhaps, one of the cleverest amateur artists in England. He is not only a painter, but a modeller and sculptor. The doorways and fireplaces of the house had been originally of granite, with torus mouldings in a style peculiar, as it appeared to us, to those parts of Devonshire where granite was used as the master stone-work of buildings. These granite door-cases and chimney-pieces had in this house, as in Monadon House which we saw in the neighbourhood of Plymouth, been covered over with plaster, we suppose to give the house a more modern air; but Mr. Bulteel has removed all this, and is restoring these leading features to their original grandeur and simplicity. The ultimate effect will be unique. There are some large rooms admirably managed both in their finishing and furniture, and a long picture gallery, with a number of curious and valuable statues and pictures. Little or nothing has yet been done to the grounds; but they possess remarkably fine features, which will, doubtless, be taken advantage of. We learned here from Mr. Bulteel that the best apple for cider is called the white-sour; and also that the custom mentioned in our *Arboretum* still exists, of addressing the apple trees at a particular season, but with some additions as follows, the additions being in italic: —

"Here's to thee, old apple tree, Whence thou mayst bud, and whence thou mayst blow; And whence thou mayst bear apples enow. Hats full! caps full! Bushel — bushel — sacks full! And my pockets full too! *If thee does not bear either apple or corn, We'll down with thy top, and up with a horn.*"

Here the farmer shoots at the tree.

Mr. Bulteel informed us that this practice is still continued by some persons; and that a few years ago a farmer, who was in the habit of going through the ridiculous ceremony, was cited before the ecclesiastical court for witchcraft; and that, before he could disentangle himself from the net in which he had inadvertently been caught, it required a considerable outlay both of time and money.

KITLEY – 'THIS IS AN EXTENSIVE AND WELL-WOODED PLACE WITH A FINE
EXPANSE OF WATER.'

KITLEY; E.P. BASTARD, ESQ.; at present in the occupation of Lord Seaton. This is an extensive and well-wooded place, with a fine expanse of water. The house has recently been improved in the old English style by George Repton, Esq.; and the flower-garden, Lord Seaton informed us, is from a design volunteered by Chantrey, while he was on a visit to the late Mr. Bastard. The drive round the park is remarkably fine, both from its trees and from its views. Beautiful views of the salt-water lake and estuary are obtained in some places, and of the open sea in others. In one part of the drive, where it passes through old quarries, the ground, the road, and the larches have been so arranged as to remind us of Switzerland; and, in other low damp places, the continuity of spruce firs of different ages recalls to mind the forests of this tree between Memel and Konigsburg. We went to the kitchen-garden to see the Kitley shaddock; but Mr. Saunders was not at home, and we could only guess at which was the plant which yielded the fruit sent to us in 1826, the first year of the *Gardener's Magazine.* In the drive we noticed a common laurel with a straight erect stem, 50ft. high, and the stem 18in. in diameter.

SALTRAM; EARL OF MORLEY. The park is very extensive and judiciously planted, and in the kitchen-garden are some good orange trees against the walls; and myrtles, magnolias, acacias, &c., as standards. The park was planted and the roads laid out, we were informed, by the late Mr. David Smith, who was the late Lord Morley's gardener for thirty-five years, and was considered one of the best gardeners of his time. He died a few months ago; and we should be glad if his widow, or some of his friends would enable us to pay a better tribute to his memory.

SEPTEMBER 13. — *MOUNT EDGECUMBE; THE EARL OF MOUNT EDGECUMBE.* We first walked through the separate gardens and all the scenes through which we could not drive; and next, in consequence of permission kindly obtained for us by Mr. Pontey, we drove through every part of the park, so that we had the great satisfaction of seeing Mount Edgecumbe deliberately and thoroughly. High as were our expectations from the published descriptions and the long celebrity of the place, we were not disappointed. We never before looked down on the sea, on shipping, and on a large town, all at our feet, from such a stupendous height. The effect on the mind is sublime in the highest degree, but yet blended with the beautiful. There was something to us quite unearthly in the feeling it created. The separate gardens, as may be readily supposed, are overgrown, and the magnolias and other fine trees greatly injured, by the elms and other common trees and shrubs. One garden, in imitation of an ancient Roman burying-ground, which contains a great many altars and urns, is so covered with evergreens, that it is not even mentioned in the guide-book. The only garden worth notice is what is called the Italian garden, though there is nothing Italian in it but the orange trees and a few white painted leaden statues; the former disfigured by the ugly unarchitectural tubs, and the latter, with the exception of a few on the parapets of a flight of steps, unartistically placed.

SEPTEMBER 14. — *PLYMOUTH TO SALTASH, TREMATON CASTLE, PENTILLIE CASTLE , AND CALLINGTON.* We found the Globe Inn at Plymouth an excellent house, centrally situated for the nurseries and the post-office, with a piano in the sitting-room, and some books, but not enough. Every inn ought to have the history and description of the town in which it is situated, if there is one; and, next, county descriptions and histories, with a copy of Shakespeare.

MOUNT EDGECUMBE – 'WE NEVER BEFORE LOOKED DOWN ON THE SEA, ON
SHIPPING AND ON A LARGE TOWN, ALL AT OUR FEET, FROM SUCH A
STUPENDOUS HEIGHT. THE EFFECT ON THE MIND IS SUBLIME IN THE HIGHEST
DEGREE BUT YET BLENDED WITH THE BEAUTIFUL.'

PENTILLIE CASTLE – 'A SPLENDID PLACE BY NATURE AND NEXT IN OUR OPINION
TO MOUNT EDGECUMBE.'

PENTILLIE CASTLE; J. T. CORYTON, ESQ. A splendid place by nature, and next in our opinion to Mount Edgecumbe. The house is particularly well situated, and entered in a proper manner, so as just to give an idea that a view of something grand and striking may be obtained from the drawingroom windows, but not to show it till there. There are some extensive walks well laid out under the direction of the late Mrs. Coryton, who, the gardener informed us, was a lady of great taste in landscape-gardening. The walks here are covered with debris from the lead and copper mines, and those which have been laid with this material twenty years ago never bear a weed, not even moss; but, on those which have been covered more recently, weeds grow the second year, because the miners are now more careful in separating the ore. At the house are some fine magnolias and large myrtles. The head-gardener has been here fifty years, and is eighty years old. We walked to a mausoleum placed on what is called Mount Ararat, in which one of the proprietors of this place is said to be interred in full dress.

244

ENDSLEIGH COTTAGE – 'WE ADMIRE ENDSLEIGH EXCEEDINGLY, FOR ITS NATURAL BEAUTIES, AND FOR THE VERY HIGH KEEPING DISPLAYED IN ALL THAT WE SAW.'

ENDSLEIGH; THE DUKE OF BEDFORD. At the entrance there is the largest, most ornamental, and best kept lodge-garden we have yet seen in Devonshire, and which may be described as characteristic of all the lodges to the Duke of Bedford's residences. Proceeding along the approach, we pass another splendid cottage-garden, the low wooden fence beautifully covered with different-coloured nasturtiums varied by dahlias. This cottage is occupied by Mr. Forester, who has the general charge of the demesne.

A little beyond this cottage we obtain the first glance at the Tamar, here a clear and rapid river, passing through richly wooded banks and fertile meadows. "The cottage on the banks of the Tamar" is not now thatched, as represented in Repton's works, and as it was when he laid out the grounds, but slated; and, though it still maintains the character of a cottage, it is, without doubt, a very commodious dwelling. Mr. Repton's description of the situation and his improvements, is calculated to give such a clear idea of the place, that, as we have at present little time, we gladly refer to it. We admire Endsleigh exceedingly, for its natural beauties, and for the very high keeping displayed in all that we saw. Over a fountain in the stable yard is the following inscription: — "Endsleigh cottage was built, and a residence created in this sequestered valley, by John Duke of Bedford; the spot having been previously chosen, from the natural picturesque beauties which surround it, by Georgiana Duchess of Bedford. The first stone of the building was laid by her four elder sons, Wriothesley, Edward, Charles Fox, and Francis John, Sept.7. 1810."

SEPTEMBER 17 — MORETON HAMPSTEAD TO UGBROOK AND EXETER. The road to Ugbrook is through a beautiful country chiefly along the sides of well-wooded valleys, with rich meadows, and apple orchards laden with fruit.

UGBROOK; LORD CLIFFORD. The park here contains the greatest quantity of fine old wood that we have seen in Devonshire. The trees are not crowded, and many of them, therefore, have attained an immense size, and taken their natural shapes.

September 18 — Exeter. Viewing the cathedral and other objects in the town.

September 19, and 20.—Bicton; Lady Rolle. This is an extensive place, celebrated for its improvements, for the collection of rare plants of every kind, for its arboretum on a large scale recently planted, and for its very high keeping. Too much can hardly be said in honour of the late Lord Rolle, through whose munificence the improvements were made, or of the present Lady Rolle, by whose taste and energetic mind His Lordship was stimulated to do so much; and, by whom, since His Lordship's death, the improvements have been continued, and the place kept up with a degree of care very rarely to be met with in similar cases.

The surface on the grounds at Bicton would be described as greatly varied in any other English county than Devonshire, but even in that picturesque county they contain many striking beauties. The park is situated within 2½ miles of the sea, of which from various points it affords fine views; and in the interior the landscape is bounded by ranges of hills, some of which are covered with wood, others with cultivated fields, and some are in a wild state. The soil is chiefly sand and sandy loam. The house, which is well placed on a knoll, is extensive and commodious, containing a suite of magnificent apartments on the principal floor, and very extensive offices, but without any pretensions to architecture.

Nothing can be more perfect than the style in which every part of this arboretum is kept; Messrs. Veitch and Son having six men constantly employed mowing the grass, and mulching the dug circles round the plants with it, as practised in the Derby Arboretum; destroying weeds as soon as they appear; and removing dead leaves, suckers from grafted plants, insects, decayed blossoms, &c. One great beauty of the Bicton arboretum is, that every tree and shrub which it contains may be seen, and the name on its label read, by a person while sitting in a carriage, and driving through it along the green walk.

There is a drive through a pine wood to a prospect tower, (the latter the best piece of architecture at Bicton,) which deserves notice for its extent and the quantity of evergreens, such as rhododendrons, mahonias, and *Ruscus aculeatus*, which have been planted as undergrowths. A great many rare pines, firs, cypresses, and junipers have also been introduced along this drive, so that, by adding more, it will in a short time be interesting as a pinetum. The tower is in the Gothic style, so high as to command a panoramic view of the surrounding country and the sea. It contains several rooms; in one of which, appropriately fitted up, a rich collection of china is tastefully displayed. This tower is understood to have been built by Lady Rolle, entirely unknown to Lord Rolle, and undiscovered by him, as an agreeable surprise for his birth-day, October 16. 1839, when he completed his 88th year; and, the following birth-day, Lady Rolle surprised Lord Rolle with the china room.

Connected with the arboretum, so as to form a part of the tour of the place, is a menagerie containing a rich collection of birds, monkeys, kangaroos, and various other foreign animals. Thus, with the arboretum, the drive to the tower, and the flower-garden, as means of recreation in the open air; the menagerie and the collection of china, for amusement under cover; and the library and pictures in the house, there is at Bicton every source of enjoyment that can be desired. Nothing is wanting but a collection of shells and minerals, for the sake of those who are fond of these departments of science, and this is about to be formed; a great quantity of shells, and some minerals, having been procured for the purpose, though they are not yet arranged.

EPILOGUE

In his early tours for *The Gardener's Magazine* John Loudon had found much neglect in the countryside, especially on the estates of the 'old' aristocracy where it resulted from absentee-ism of landowners and a reduction in workforces. The villa residences of the middle classes were better maintained. In Loudon's later travels, whether as a result of his exhortations or not, there had been improvements in the upkeep of the land.

Paradoxically, it is the great estates of the aristocracy, many of which were in such dire straights in Loudon's time, that have lasted best in the long-term. Survival has been achieved by learning, maybe initially at Loudon's instigations, to adapt to altered and altering circumstances – even Safari Parks. Bad times have toughened the sinews of those on the land; there was another major agricultural depression in the 1870s and the effects of the two World Wars in this century were similar to those of the Napoleonic Wars chronicled by Loudon. Most of the large houses and parks he described are now in good heart; whereas the homes of the then bourgeoisie may now be so engulfed by the very urban sprawl that their original owners helped to create, that they are unrecognizable.

It is not easy now to assess the importance of John Claudius Loudon in his time. But the views of his peers can help our appreciation of him. His contemporary, Joseph Paxton, joint-editor of the *Horticultural Register*, said this of Loudon: 'During the earlier part of his literary career, his strictures, etc were often severe, and caused some offence. This will almost necessarily be the case with a man of integrity who sets out in the endeavour to correct great existing evils.' Nevertheless, Paxton opined that with *The Gardener's Magazine* Loudon had 'created a new era in gardening'.

Another editor of a rival publication, the *Horticultural Journal*, George Glenny wrote in an obituary for the *Gardener's Gazette*: 'Mr Loudon, as a public writer on gardening, entertained and promulgated singular notions; but, of all the authors on the subject, he was unquestionably the most patient, pains-taking and persevering, that ever produced a book'. In the *Derby Reporter*, one of Loudon's draughtsmen commented: 'Mr Loudon's love of truth, like that of every great and good man, was perfect . . . Mr Loudon also mixed with his love of truth, determination . . . His love of order was also very great'.

That Loudon was a man of integrity and diligence is demonstrated. But did he actually influence gardening practice? Was he the arbiter of taste and instrument of reform that he so clearly wished to be or merely an opinionated busybody?

Jane Loudon in her memoir written after her husband's death, described *The Gardener's Magazine* as 'the organ through which he communicated his own thoughts and feelings to the public'. So, apparently, through its pages Loudon himself believed he was revealed. Perhaps, by reading them, we can determine whether it is because of John Claudius Loudon's groundwork in the nineteenth century that we have become a nation of gardeners today.

CKNOWLEDGEMENTS

AND

INDEX

The creation of this book has involved the assistance of many people, organizations and official bodies throughout Britain, all of whom have been courteous and helpful when confronted with detailed requests for information and the whereabouts of specific illustrations. We wish to thank the following for their considerable contribution.

S.J. Barnes; Michael Bott; P.J. Broughton; Gordon Brookes; Sarah Brown; David Burns; G.D. Bye; Stephen Croad; W.J. Crow; C. Cruft; C.R. Davey; Breat Elliot; D.V. Fowkes; Patricia Gill; John Gower; M. Gower; J.A.S. Green; Valerie Griffith; H.A. Hanley; H. Jaques; Cynthia Graham Kerr; Martin Knebel; G.A. Knight; I.C. Laurie; Ian Lawley; Nigel K. Lutt; M.S.J. MacPherson; Christine North; Daphne Phillips; C. Pickford; John G. Rhodes; M.M. Rowe; Kay N. Sanecki; Derek M.M. Shorrocks; Elizabeth Stuart; M.D. Trace; C.R. St. Q. Wall; David Wall; Peter Walne; Marilyn Ward; Lavinia Wellicome; I. White; L. White.

The Staff of the County Archives, Local History Collections and Libraries in Bedfordshire; Buckinghamshire; Cheshire; Cornwall; Derbyshire; Devonshire; Hampshire; Hertfordshire; Lincolnshire; Middlesex; Oxfordshire; Somerset; Staffordshire; Sussex and Wiltshire. Thanks, too, to The Royal Horticultural Society; The Royal Botanic Gardens, Kew; the Linnean Society; The Ministry of Agriculture Library; and The Minet Library.

The Publishers wish to thank the following for permission to reproduce material in this book:

BLACK AND WHITE

The Syndics of Cambridge University Library (14, 17, 22, 37, 41, 51, 54, 60, 61, 64, 71, 80, 95, 100, 111, 115, 119, 136, 140(above), 141, 142, 149, 150, 151, 154, 156, 178, 183, 194, 195, 196, 235, 236, 245); Hertfordshire Record Office (21, 158, 159, 160, 161, 162, 163, 164, 170, 173, 174); Bedfordshire County Record Office (23); The Minet Library (31, 32(below)); The Royal Commission on the Historical Monuments of England (39, 43, 44, 59, 62, 69, 70, 72, 94, 112, 113, 144, 172, 181, 200, 234, 243); His Grace the Duke of Norfolk (42); Stowe School (55, 56); B.E.C. Howarth-Loomes (57, 179, 180, 184, 199, 239); Warwick County Record Office (58); City Museums, Stoke-on-Trent (70, 201, 202); D. Sherborn (81); Berkshire County Record Office (97, 98, 99); Hampshire County Council (104); Oxfordshire County Libraries (116/117, 121, 123, 129, 130), E. de Rothschild, Esq. (133, 134, 135); W.R. Allen (140(below)); Salisbury and South Wiltshire Museum (155); British Architectural Library RIBA London (171); Country Life (191, 192, 193); Royal Commission on the Ancient and Historical Monuments of Scotland (213, 214, 215, 216, 217, 218, 222, 223); Devon Library Services (240, 242); Cornwall Record Office (244).

COLOUR

25 From Knowsley's expanded edition c. 1832 of Clutterbuck's *History of Hertfordshire,* originally published in 3 volumes 1815-1827. – Courtesy of Hertfordshire Record Office. (H.R.O.); 26-7 Witherington *(The Fête at Petworth Park) c.* 1835 – Courtesy of The National Trust. (N.T.); 28(i) Artist unknown, *Goodwood;* *The Temple c.* 1850 28(ii) Artist unknown, *Goodwood; A View from the Old Grandstand c.* 1850 – From Goodwood House by courtesy of the Trustees; 45 From W.H. Bartlett and W. Penry; *A Series of Drawings, Illustrative of the Scenery and Architecture of the Deepdene, Surrey, the seat of Thomas Hope, Esquire, made in the year 1825.* An album in the possession of the Minet Library. – Courtesy of The London Borough of Lambeth Archives Department. (L.A.D.); 46 From Bartlett and Penry *op. cit.* (L.A.D.); 47 From Bartlett and Penry *op. cit.* (L.A.D.); 48(i) From Bartlett and Penry *op. cit.* (L.A.D.); 48(ii) From Bartlett and Penry *op. cit.* (L.A.D.); 65 Artist unknown, possibly L.J. Wood, *Alton Station c.* 1840. (detail) – Courtesy of The Trustees of The William Salt Library. (W.S.L.); 66-7 From E. Adveno Brooke, *The Gardens of England,* 1857. – Courtesy of the Syndics of Cambridge University Library. (C.U.L.); 68(i) From E. Adveno Brooke *op. cit.* (C.U.L.); 68(ii) E. Adveno Brooke, *The Green Bough, Staffordshire,* date unknown. (W.S.L.); 85 From Jane Loudon, *The Ladies' Flower-Garden of Ornamental Greenhouse Plants,* 1848. – By courtesy of The Trustees of the Royal Botanic Gardens, Kew. (R.B.G. Kew.); 86-7 George Pickering, *The Rock Garden At Hoole House, c.* 1830. – By courtesy of The Grosvenor Museum, Chester; 88 From Lawson, *The Pinetum Britannicum.* (R.B.G. Kew.); 105 From Jane Loudon, *The Ladies' Flower-Garden of Ornamental Bulbous Plants, 1841.* (R.B.G. Kew.); 106 From Lawson, *op. cit.* (R.B.G. Kew.); 107 From Jane Loudon, *The Ladies' Flower-Garden of Ornamental Annuals,* 1844. (R.B.G. Kew.); 108 From Jane

Loudon, *The Ladies' Flower-Garden of Ornamental Greenhouse Plants,* 1848. (R.B.G. Kew.); 125 From Jane Loudon, *The Ladies' Flower-Garden of Ornamental Bulbous Plants,* 1841. (R.B.G. Kew.); 126-7 Artist Unknown, *The Gardens at Stourhead c.* 1780 (N.T.); 128 From M. Drapier, *Herbier de l'Amateur de Fleurs,* vol.6, 1833. (R.B.G. Kew.); 145 J.B. Knight, *Wardour Castle and Fonthill Abbey, c.*1825. – Courtesy of the Salisbury and South Wiltshire Museum; 146-7 From E. Adveno Brooke, *op. cit.* (C.U.L.); 148 From Knowsley, *op. cit.* (H.R.O.); 165 From M. Drapier, *op. cit.* vol.3, 1829. (R.G.B. Kew.); 166-7 From Knowsley, *op. cit.* (H.R.O.); 168(i) From E. Adveno Brooke, *op. cit.* (C.U.L.); 168(ii) From Knowsley, *op. cit.* (H.R.O.); 185 From E. Adveno Brook, *op. cit.* (C.U.L.); 186-7 From Knowsley, *op. cit.* (H.R.O.); 188 From Knowsley, *op. cit.* (H.R.O.); 197 E. Adveno Brooke, *Park Lane by Trentham Hall, Staffs,* date unknown. (detail) (W.S.L.); 198 E. Adveno Brooke, *View near Handford, Staffs,* date unknown. (detail) (W.S.L.); 207 From E. Adveno Brooke, *op. cit.* (C.U.L.); 208-9 From E. Adveno Brooke, *op. cit.* (C.U.L.); 210(i) From E. Adveno Brooke, *op. cit.* (C.U.L.); 210(ii) From E. Adveno Brooke, *op. cit.* (C.U.L.); 219 P. Sandby *Bothwell Castle* date unknown (detail) – Courtesy of The National Gallery of Scotland. (N.G.S.); 220 James Ward, *Melrose Abbey c.* 1807 (detail) (N.G.S.); 229 From Lawson, *op. cit.* (R.B.G. Kew.); 230-1 Philip Rogers, *Saltram* before 1820. (N.T.); 232 From Lawson, *op. cit.* (R.B.G. Kew.).